Your Child: Bully or Victim?

Understanding and Ending School Yard Tyranny

by

Peter Sheras, Ph.D.

with Sherill Tippins

A Skylight Press Book

FIRESIDE

NEW YORK LONDON TORONTO

SYDNEY SINGAPORE

Copyright © 2002 by Peter Sheras, Ph.D., and Skylight Press

A Skylight Press Book

FIRESIDE and colophon are registered trademarks
of Simon & Schuster, Inc.

For information regarding special discounts for bulk purchases,
please contact Simon & Schuster Special Sales:
1-800-456-6798 or business@simonandschuster.com

Designed by Christine Weathersbee

Manufactured in the United States of America

10 9 8 7 6 5 4 3 2 1

Library of Congress Cataloging-in-Publication Data

Sheras, Peter L.
Your child : bully or victim? : understanding and ending
school yard tyranny / by Peter Sheras with Sherill Tippins.
        p.   cm.
"A fireside book."
Includes index.
1. School violence—Prevention.   2. Bullying—Prevention.
        I. Tippin, Sherill.   II. Title.
            LB3013.3 .S49 2002
371.5'8—dc21   2002022160
            ISBN 0-7432-2923-1

This book is dedicated to my caring wife,
Phyllis, and my loving children,
Daniel and Sarah

I further dedicate this work
to my late friend and colleague,
Joseph B. Tavormina
(1949–1979)

ACKNOWLEDGMENTS

A book such as this does not come about without support from others. Special thanks go to Andrea Levy, my student and assistant on this project. I gratefully acknowledge the help of Dewey Cornell, Ph.D., and the members of the Virginia Youth Violence Project at the University of Virginia. Finally I wish to thank my wife, Phyllis Koch-Sheras, for her love, support and advice.

CONTENTS

Your Child:
Bully or Victim?

CHAPTER ONE

THE ROOTS OF
AGGRESSION

Eight-year-old Michael, new to the neighborhood, comes home from school each day with a new bruise or rip in his clothes. Ten-year-old Emily frequently goes without lunch because a group of her classmates keep trashing her lunch bag. Twelve-year-old Angela finds her name posted on the Internet in a list of "Fat Slobs of Northside Middle School." Fourteen-year-old Deborah, sexually assaulted at a party her parents don't know she attended, is considering suicide as a way to escape the gossips at school. Sixteen-year-old Henry, sick of the daily taunts of "faggot" from neighborhood kids, has started checking periodically to see whether his dad has locked up the ammo for his gun.

If your child is being bullied at school, in your neighborhood or even at home, you know it is no laughing matter. Your child may be getting off the school bus in tears, writing furiously in a journal or spending weekends alone when other kids are out having fun. He may have experienced nightmares, a drop in grades, or a sudden change from an eager, optimistic student to a depressed, under-achieving loner. If so, his experience is by no means unique. Nearly every school-aged child in America has witnessed or experienced, or will soon experience, bullying in some form or another. Every two seconds of every school day, according to the National Education Association, another student is physically attacked in school. A typical schoolchild has a nearly 25 percent chance of being involved in bullying on campus, taunting on the bus, sexual harassment, "flaming" on the Internet, beatings or gang activity. One in every five students will bring a weapon to school at some point. According to a recent survey, even in *elementary school*, personal harm or attack by others is the students' most frequent and intense worry. It is hardly surprising, then, that the National Education Association reports an estimated 160,000 students missing school every day specifically to avoid being bullied.

THE TROUBLE WITH BULLYING

In recent years, a series of violent incidents have brought the issue of bullying to the center of parents' and educators' attention. In 1999, two teenagers who had suffered years of taunts and insults gunned down thirteen fellow students at Colorado's Columbine High School before taking their own lives. In 2001, a bullied fourteen-year-old student at California's Santana High killed two classmates and injured thirteen. These along with additional recent shootings, suicides and other acts of extreme violence have awakened many parents, educators and other adults to the fact that bullying is not an inevitable rite of passage or a harmless part of growing up.

The response has been galvanizing. Emergency hotlines and support groups have been created for bullying victims and their families. Educators have developed curricula that address issues of cruelty among children, and school administrators have instituted zero-tolerance policies regarding physical, sexual, racial and other forms of abuse. A number of psychologists, myself included, have focused on the issue of youth violence in a therapeutic setting, helping both victims and bullies find new ways to cope with anger, depression and aggressive impulses. Even legislators have responded by introducing laws in some states cracking down on harassment, hazing and violence in schools. Some of these actions have proven quite useful, others less so. What is lacking is a clear, rational understanding of what bullying is, how and why it occurs and which techniques are most effective in stopping it.

As a child in elementary school, I myself was a victim of bullying. My experience sensitized me throughout middle and high school to the plight of my classmates who were being victimized. As an undergraduate I studied psychology and sociology in an effort to understand the mind of preteens and adolescents, and focused in graduate school on adolescent group behaviors and how to change them. For the past twenty-six years, I have worked as a clinical psychologist with teenagers and their families to manage issues relating to victimization, bullying, depression and violence. In 1993, while a faculty member of the University of Virginia, I helped found and direct the Virginia Youth Violence Project. Currently, I coordinate the local school crisis network, advise federal and state government on issues relating to youth and violence and serve on a research team that evaluates anti-bullying programs in schools.

What have I learned from my experience working with bullies, victims and their families? I have learned that bullying is not a question of "bad kids versus good kids," but a situation in which *both* children need help in learning how to channel their emotions and interact successfully with others. I have learned that nearly every child has the potential to become a bully or a victim, given the right circumstances. In fact, they are often the same person, as bullies are frequently victimized by others, and victims can turn to bullying in an attempt to resolve their situation. I have learned that parents can do a great deal to prevent their children from becoming bullies, victims or even passive bystanders—but only if they take the time to understand the dynamics of bullying relationships, encourage their children's trust and confidence and intervene in effective ways when necessary.

Finally, I have learned that the key to changing the way children interact is for adults from all parts of their environment—parents, teachers, policemen, counselors and other professionals—to work together to *change the social climate* so that bullying is no longer considered an acceptable form of expression. By educating children about the different forms of bullying and its effects, encouraging their participation in setting rules prohibiting bullying and substituting more positive behaviors, and consistently enforcing limits, parents and other adults can have a powerful impact on their children's experience at home, at school and in the community.

Every child should be able to grow up in a world without oppression or bullying, and be taught to channel his aggressive impulses in socially acceptable ways. Only when our children learn to identify and respond appropriately to bullying, when we parents act to ensure our children's right to safety, and when schools and communities support that right as well, will the surge in violence among children in this country begin to abate. In this chapter, I will introduce you to some of the basic concepts relating to human aggression so that you can begin to think about how bullying occurs and consider ways to help your child manage his own and others' aggression in positive, enriching ways.

IS IT HUMAN NATURE?

One of the most frequent comments you are likely to hear about bullying is "Well, that's the way kids are and there's nothing you can do about it." But is this statement actually true? Is bullying really an innate aspect of human nature and a necessary part of growing up? To answer this question, it is first necessary to differentiate between *anger, aggression* and *bullying*. Anger is an emotion that every human being feels—an emotion that can lead to aggressive impulses. An aggressive impulse—the urge to hurt another person—can be expressed or channeled in a number of ways. Bullying—unprovoked aggressive behavior meant to dominate, hurt or exclude another— is one way to channel aggression. More acceptable ways include punching a pillow, writing in a journal or working out for thirty minutes on the basketball court.

It is this confusion among terms that often gives rise to misleading comparisons between bullying in humans and aggressive behavior in other closely related primate species. It is true that a large number of monkeys and apes use repeated, unprovoked attacks on others to reinforce their social rank, unify the group by identifying a common enemy and release frustration. The victims in these relationships resemble human scapegoats at first glance in that they are low-ranking members of the group, routinely picked on in times of stress. The difference, however, lies in human beings' ability to *vary* their behaviors in creative ways. When your child feels stressed, angry or frustrated, he can be taught to find positive solutions for his discomfort rather than automatically picking on a weaker companion. The weaker companion can learn to escape victimization by avoiding the aggressor, can deflect his aggressor's anger through assertive statements or humor or can turn to his peers or to adults for support. While apes are locked into their behaviors by a million years of evolution, humans involved in conflict can look for and practice new responses.

Other evidence that is commonly used to "prove" that bullying is inevitable is the fact that children, left to themselves, behave in decidedly aggressive and bullying ways. Toddlers routinely grab toys from other children, bite and push when they are angry and refuse to take turns. Kindergartners and elementary school children often enjoy excluding others from their groups ("No boys allowed!"). Preteens and adolescents can become masters at spreading malicious gossip, ganging up on young children and sexually harassing or labeling vulnerable peers. Much of this behavior has its roots in normal childhood development. Toddlers generally can't comprehend others' needs, desires or points of view. Kindergartners who exclude others are expressing their expanding social awareness and their fascination with figuring out who they are (girls, for example, as opposed to boys). Adolescents who gang up on others are exploring similar social issues on a more sophisticated level, and those who engage in sexual bullying are often responding to a surge in hormones.

While it is true that all of these behaviors spring from normal human development—and that many animal species exhibit similar types of social jostling as they grow—human beings are, again, capable of rechanneling these aggressive urges in more positive ways. Toddlers can be trained (over time) to use words instead of striking out, and kindergartners can learn tactful ways to limit the members of their group. Teenagers can establish and maintain social status through kindness and positive achievement instead of bullying and can find harmless ways to attract the opposite sex. The tendency toward physical, emotional or social bullying may be "natural" in some very limited sense, in other words, but it is *not* inevitable in our schools, neighborhoods and homes. In this book, I will demonstrate a number of techniques for helping your child to manage his and others' aggression and to intervene positively when necessary.

THE DYNAMICS OF ABUSE

As you try to understand and deal with your child's aggressive acts or victimization, you may find it hard to tell the difference between actual cases of bullying and everyday teasing or social jostling. You may wonder whether the aggressor is wholly at fault or the victim is contributing to the abuse in some way. I will address these issues at length in later chapters, but for now you may find it useful to consider how bullying is defined by psychologist Dan Olweus, one of the preeminent researchers in the field: a child is being bullied "when he or she is exposed, repeatedly and over time, to negative actions on the part of one or more other students." Negative actions are any physical, verbal or social action in which the bully intentionally causes injury or discomfort. In most cases, the bully is aware that the actions are painful or unpleasant.

When you are considering a situation in which your own child is involved, then, it helps to ask yourself the following:

- whether the incident has happened *repeatedly* (all children make mistakes, but bullies repeat their attacks even after the victim protests).
- whether the bully is aware that she is causing pain.
- whether the victim has made it clear that she resents the behavior.
- whether the act is playful and friendly or of a degrading or offensive nature.
- whether there is a real or perceived imbalance in strength, power or numbers between the victim and the other child or children. A bully always chooses a weaker opponent. A struggle between two equals is not bullying.

If you have answered yes to most or all of these questions, then your child is probably involved in a bullying relationship. This realization can be extremely distressing, especially if you were involved in bullying episodes when you yourself were a child. If you worry that your child is a "born bully" or a "born victim," however, it may come as a relief to know that there is no such thing. Even if your child is larger or more active than others, she can be taught to channel her energy in other ways and to accommodate others' smaller size. While your shy child or one with a behavior disorder may be at greater risk of being bullied, she can learn to compensate for these disadvantages and develop other strengths.

In fact, the reason why your child may be chosen as a victim depends to a large degree on her *perceived* strength in relation to the bully. You may assume, as did most of the schoolchildren in a recent survey, that an unusual appearance or shabby clothes will cause a student to be victimized. Research has demonstrated that this is not the case if the child's wit, friendliness, self-confidence or other social strengths compensate for her unusual looks. By the same token, a strong, good-looking boy may be victimized if his low self-esteem or poor social skills render him vulnerable. A child's "social intelligence" and level of self-esteem are the real determinants when it comes to whether or not she will be victimized.

WHAT YOU THINK YOU KNOW

Bullying situations are complex and painful and can be difficult to resolve. Parents can hardly be blamed for wishing they would just disappear. Perhaps that is the reason for the proliferation of incorrect "facts" about what causes bullying and how it should be addressed—truisms that prevent parents from taking any action at all. Many adults believe, for example, that it's best to let kids work out bullying problems on their own, without adult interference. Others assume that all it takes to discourage a bully is to hit back once or to ignore him until he goes away. You yourself may believe that if your child were being bullied he would tell you, or that if he were hurting others you would know.

Such assumptions—when you think you know more about a bullying relationship than you do—can have tragic consequences when

they prevent parents from taking action. Research has shown that
bullies whose behavior is not corrected during childhood often become criminals as adults, and that victims who fail to find relief frequently experience depression and severe drops in self-esteem that
can negatively impact their later years.

For your child's sake, take some time as you read this book to
think in greater depth about all the forms that bullying takes, how
bullies choose their victims (and what makes them stop) and how
you might be able to learn whether your child is involved in physical, emotional or sexual abuse. By looking beyond your precon-
ceptions to your child's actual experience and emotions, you can
begin to see how to effectively help your child and perhaps other
children as well. Whether your child is hurting others, is a victim
of aggression or is just a concerned bystander, your clearer understanding will enable you to help him stop the bullying before it gets
worse.

WHAT YOU CAN DO

In the chapters that follow, I will share with you accounts of many of
the bullying situations I have come across in my professional practice, my research and my own experience as a child and as a parent.
Some of these descriptions may strike a familiar note. Others may
shock or surprise you. In each case I will provide you with coping
techniques that have helped many of my clients in similar predica-
ments—techniques aimed at managing one's own and others' anger
at home and elsewhere, at improving communication among family
members and with peers and at accomplishing real change at school
and in the community. No matter how shy or frightened your child
is now—or how angry and abusive to her peers—there is much you
can do to help her manage her emotions without limiting her independence or impeding her growth. I will help you through this
process step by step by focusing on:

How to recognize bullying and understand how it happens so that you can protect your child when she needs it. A number of myths about bullying surround us, misleading us as to what causes bullying behavior; what type of child typically bullies or is bullied; whether, when and to what extent such behavior is acceptable and how to best correct it. In Chapter 2, I will examine such myths as "bullying toughens you up" and "victims are wimps," and point out the ways in which they can blind parents to the pain their children are experiencing. In Chapter 3, I will focus on the different forms that bullying can take, the social dynamics that typically lead to bullying and victimlike behavior, and the places where bullying most commonly occurs.

How to talk with and *listen to* your child in ways that will enable you to help her through a bullying situation in the most appropriate way. Most children don't easily admit to their parents that they're bullying or being bullied. In Chapters 4 and 5, I will provide you with a list of behaviors that may signal that your child is in trouble and suggest ways to talk with her about it. In Chapter 6, I will focus on how your child can intervene in bullying situations she witnesses without being bullied herself—and how you can help her to develop the courage and confidence to do so.

How to deal with a bullying situation once you know it is occurring. In Chapter 7, I will focus on ways you can empower your child to handle aggressive behavior herself. While it is important not to abandon your child to "work it out on her own," you can teach her coping mechanisms that will help her to better manage her own anger and respond productively to others'. In Chapter 8, I will discuss when, why and how you should intervene personally in a bullying situation, and examine the best way to approach a bullying child or her parents. Since so much bullying takes place at school, I will focus in Chapter 9 on specific ways to successfully intervene in situations on campus, on the bus and on the daily route to and from campus. In Chapter 10, I will explore legal, therapeutic and community remedies to bullying and victimization wherever it occurs.

How to expand on lessons in managing aggression throughout childhood and adolescence. Bullying may not be a social inevitability, but it pervades nearly every aspect of our culture. In Chapter 11, I will explore ways in which the lessons learned in combating aggression during childhood or adolescence can improve your son's or daughter's life (and perhaps yours) throughout the decades to come.

No one who was involved in taunting, beating, ostracism or other acts of cruelty during childhood ever forgets how painful it can be. Even now, as an adult, you may continue to dream of getting revenge or apologizing for those past pains. You may even be struggling with the same patterns of behavior in your current life. If so, you understand more than other parents how urgently any child entangled in an abusive situation, whether bully or victim, needs help. Ultimately, in this book, I hope to offer a glimpse of the complex web of problems, concerns, fears and conflicts that children and adolescents face, as well as the frequently unsteady support systems that characterize their world. Together, we will explore how and why we need to make the effort to understand these issues, help our children express their feelings about them and then act constructively to protect the well-being of our families.

CHAPTER TWO

"KIDS WILL BE KIDS" AND OTHER MYTHS ABOUT BULLYING

OUR CULTURE IS PERMEATED with myths about bullying—misconceptions that make it possible to ignore physical, emotional and social cruelty even as it takes place right in front of us. Some of this "folk wisdom" addresses the nature or purpose of bullying (it's a natural process that weeds out the weak and allows the fittest to survive; it's a necessary part of learning to survive in the real world). Some myths provide comfortable categories or stereotypes of bullies and victims (bullies are social outcasts, victims "ask for it" through their social ineptitude). Others promote adults' powerlessness to change the situation for the better (kids have to handle this on their own).

None of these myths is true, yet, as is the case with many other stereotypes, each contains a kernel of validity—enough to keep many adults from fully considering their child's situation. As we discussed in Chapter 1, for example, a certain level of jostling for social position in a group *is* a natural and inevitable part of childhood (and human social interaction in general). It is not true, however, that

12

such social competition must turn violent or destructive. Bullying has nothing to do with everyday social maneuvering and everything to do with the bully's inability to properly channel his feelings of frustration or rage.

What happens when we parents allow ourselves to believe these myths? Typically, we offer our children the usual advice ("Ignore them, honey. This happens all the time. They'll move on to someone else soon.") and consider the subject closed. Our reliance on such general truisms blinds us to the truth of what is actually happening to our children, and we fail to listen clearly to what they tell us. A child who is advised to ignore a bully probably suspects that this advice is not that helpful—and she is right. Study after study has demonstrated that ignoring a bully is likely to lead to an increase in the level of violence. Yet when she follows her parents' or other adults' advice and the harassment continues, she is likely to decide that it is her fault that she is being bullied. She stops asking for help from adults, since it has had no effect. She feels isolated with her problem and alienated from adults, with nowhere to turn. As the attacks continue, her self-esteem plunges, her frustration increases and her emotional, social and academic health worsen as a result.

Victims of bullying are not the only ones who suffer from the prevalence of such misleading assumptions. Bullies, too, are often incorrectly stereotyped—as "bad seeds," "social outcasts" and "juvenile delinquents" from broken homes. As we will see in this chapter, children become bullies for a wide variety of reasons and have a wide range of backgrounds. Many are quite popular, many come from "good families," and most are capable of learning to rechannel their anger or fear of rejection more effectively if offered appropriate training and reinforcement. In other words, bullying is not simply a bad-guys-versus-good-guys situation. It is a complex behavioral problem between individuals—sometimes instigated by the bully alone but occasionally created or magnified by bully and victim together. Only by shedding our culture's simplistic assumptions can we adults help untangle the conflict and show both bully and victim a better way to interact.

In this chapter, we will examine some of the more common myths regarding the function and effects of bullying in childhood, the types of children who tend to bully others or are victimized and how bullying can best be addressed. But first, it may be instructive to take the following quiz to learn more about your own assumptions and where they might lead when trying to help your own child.

TEST YOUR BULLY IQ

1. *Most of the time, what kids call bullying is just run-of-the-mill teasing.*

   FALSE. Kids are usually aware of the difference between playful teasing and deliberate bullying. Rarely will they complain to a parent if the teasing is "all in good fun." Kidding around becomes bullying when the instigator refuses to stop even after her target protests or it otherwise becomes clear that she is causing real pain. It is also helpful to remember that friendly teasing takes place among equals, while verbal or other types of bullying occur between two children who are unequal in age, size, social status or some other form of power.

2. *It's the teacher's responsibility to make sure that bullying doesn't happen at school.*

   TRUE AND FALSE. Certainly, it is the teacher's responsibility to refuse to tolerate bullying and to stop it when she sees it happening. In too many instances, teachers make use of the cultural myths described in this chapter to justify ignoring abusive behavior in the class-room. It must be acknowledged, however, that much school-related bullying behavior takes place outside the classroom (such as on the playground and school bus), where teachers may not see it. If bullying is to be curbed, parents, teachers, school administrators and other adults must work together, *as a team*, to prevent abuse wherever it happens.

3. ***There's no point in trying to talk about the problem with a bully's parents. Bullies' parents never listen.***

    FALSE. Like any stereotype, the image of a bully's par-ents as ignorant and abusive themselves may be correct in some instances and completely wrong in others. Children engage in bullying behavior for a number of reasons: peer pressure, temporary stress, a reaction to having been bullied by other children or a need to win their parents' attention—as well as because bullying is what they experience at home. A bully's parents may be well meaning but utterly unaware that their child is ex-periencing pain and expressing it in violent ways. In these cases, they are likely to be grateful to any adult who offers to work with them to begin to solve this problem.

4. ***Some people are born bullies and there's nothing you can do about it.***

    FALSE. This assumption is based on the fact that chil-dren are born with different personalities or tempera-ments—each possessing her own energy level, degree of social openness or inhibition and level of aggression. This does not mean, however, that some children are "born bullies." Even a child who is larger, more dominating or more impulsive than her peers can be taught to channel that energy in nonabusive ways.

5. *Some people are born victims who will always be picked on.*

    FALSE. Since bullies always choose as their target a child who is in some way less powerful than they are, it may seem at first that a child who is physically smaller, socially less adept or otherwise not on a par with her peers will inevitably become a victim. Yet studies have shown that far more important than any apparent disadvantage is the child's *perception* of her strength in relation to the bully. A child who is smaller, plumper or less well dressed than her peers can nevertheless hold her own if she feels empowered through experiences in other aspects of life and supported by the adults in her environment.

6. *A victim is never a bully.*

    FALSE. Recent surveys report that roughly 40 percent of victims admit to having bullied others themselves. In some cases, a child's bullying and victimlike behaviors both stem from the same emotional difficulties or lack of social skills. In many cases, victims who have found no one to help them turn to bullying as a way of expressing their anger and attempting to escape their role as scapegoat. Bully-victims' deep feelings of rage and alienation make them the most likely children to turn to extreme forms of violence, including murder.

HOW BULLYING WORKS

No adult enjoys hearing about abuse among children. It is almost physically painful to imagine our children being beaten up, taunted or otherwise harassed by their peers. Descriptions of bullying bring back memories from our own childhood that we would prefer to forget. Bullying situations are almost always complicated—requiring adults to try to judge how serious the abuse is, how best to address it and how to tell if the bullying has really stopped. It is perhaps understandable, then, that myths about the basic nature of bullying and the role it plays in children's lives are so widely accepted. By calling bullying normal we absolve ourselves of responsibility and leave another generation to struggle through on its own.

Following are a number of case histories involving bullying, accompanied by a discussion of a variety of cultural assumptions that may have helped determine their outcome. As you read these accounts, take some time to consider your own child's situation and how it might have been similarly affected.

Myth 1. Bullying toughens a child up.

Janeen had always been shy and preferred to play alone. She was terribly self-conscious about her slight overbite, and as adolescence approached she seemed increasingly ill at ease in her tall, gangly body. Her parents, Adrienne and George, hoped she would find new friends and a fresh start as she entered the neighborhood's large new middle school that fall. To prepare, Adrienne bought her daughter several new outfits and talked a lot about all the fun things that teenaged girls get to do. Soon, Janeen herself started to look a little optimistic, and to bolster her daughter's positive feelings Adrienne fought the temptation to remind her to stand straight, hold her head up and smile more often.

Once school began, Janeen's parents waited eagerly for news of her success, but when they asked how things were going, she usually just muttered "Fine," before going to her room and shutting the door. Then one day, several weeks into the school year, she arrived home in tears. "Some big guys on the bus were teasing me," she told her mother, wiping her eyes. "They called me names."

Listening to her daughter, Adrienne fought back anger, anxiety and impatience. Uncomfortable memories from her own adolescence added to her mix of emotions and left her wanting to shake her daughter as well as comfort her. *Why does she let people treat her like that?* she asked herself. *Why doesn't she fight back? Look at her— walking around slumped and gloomy, just like a victim. No wonder the boys treat her that way.* When George heard what happened over dinner that night, he reacted similarly. "Just ignore them. Sit somewhere else on the bus," he told his daughter impatiently. "Bullies are something you're going to have to learn to deal with. You're going to run into them all your life." To his wife he added later, "She could use toughening up. Maybe dealing with this situation will snap her out of her shyness. We've been babying her for too long."

Adrienne and George heard no more about the boys from their daughter after that. In fact, they didn't hear much of anything from her. Janeen went straight from school to her room and spoke mainly in monosyllables at dinner. By the end of the first semester, her grades had plummeted. As far as Adrienne could tell, she had made no friends. A couple of times she had come home with rips on her clothes, but she denied that anything was wrong.

Was Janeen all right? her parents wondered. Was this just part of the normal "blue period" of adolescence? Or was their daughter in trouble? George and Adrienne wished they could get their daughter to open up about her experiences, but the more they pressed her to talk with them, the more closemouthed and resentful she became.

Adolescence is a difficult time for all children and their parents, and it is hard to know when to actively help a child with his problems and when to encourage him to deal with them himself. Just as we wondered when our children were younger whether they would ever learn to use their napkins at the table and stop eating with their hands, so we feel impatient when we see our older children and adolescents succumb to teasing or allow others to continually beat, harass or otherwise torment them. Yet so often parents fail to understand that, just as they had to teach their children proper table manners, so they must show their children *how* to resist bullying and interact with others more positively. Without adult attention and correction—for both victim and bully—children will continue to flounder in destructive patterns that they cannot escape.

No other form of harassment is as socially acceptable as bullying. Racism and sexism are rarely tolerated. Stalking, assault and molestation are all against the law. Yet bullying, which has been shown to create serious, lasting physical and emotional damage to children, continues to be tolerated as a "character builder." Far from toughening a child up, bullying much more often leads to academic failure, depression, physical damage and even, in some cases, extreme violence against oneself or others. If a child were drowning in a swimming pool, calling for help, we would dive in and save him. If he comes home in tears from a beating or taunting, he needs immediate help as well.

Myth 2. It's just a phase. They'll grow out of it. After all, kids will be kids.

Brian was small for his age, and in early grades he was frequently teased and bullied. In high school, however, he discovered that there was power in numbers. He joined a gang of older teenagers who enjoyed picking on younger kids, forcing them to hand over their lunch money and other items.

When Brian's parents first received reports from school that their son had been involved in such behavior, they couldn't help feeling a little relieved that, for once, Brian was not the one being picked on. They were also glad to hear that, while Brian had been part of the group who harassed other children, he had not been accused of doing any stealing himself. They sternly told Brian to leave the younger kids alone and grounded him for a week. "It's just a stage," his father assured his wife that night. "They have to try out behavior like that. Brian will drop it soon enough."

But Brian's behavior didn't stop. According to the reports that continued to arrive, Brian's gang of friends was becoming involved in increasingly serious acts of violence. There were accusations that a boy had been beaten up, and a girl claimed that several of the boys had cornered and threatened her. Brian denied having been involved in these incidents, however, and his parents believed him. He was simply too small to scare anyone, they thought.

"This school is really getting hysterical," Brian's mother remarked one evening as she read an announcement about a new zero-tolerance policy regarding bullying on campus. "Aren't kids allowed to be kids anymore?"

Because Brian's parents refused to take his bullying seriously, it came as a shock when he was arrested a month before he would have graduated from high school. It seemed that Brian and several of his friends had ganged up on the clerk at a convenience store, tied him up, locked him in the storeroom and stolen all the cash from the cash register. "How did this happen?" his mother demanded as she and her husband scrambled to post bail. "He was doing fine! He had friends. He was on the football team. How could he have ended up here?"

Particularly in this country, where independence and self-sufficiency are so prized, many parents tend to look the other way when they hear that their child is either the victim or perpetrator of teasing, taunting, ambushing or other forms of cruelty. Recalling their own experiences with bullying, they assume that such behavior is a normal part of childhood that, like pimples or puppy love, will eventually be outgrown. Again, this error in judgment results from confusion between the more benign forms of teasing—which occur only on occasion between children who are roughly equal in power and are not intended to cause pain—and true bullying, which is more chronic and deliberate in nature and results in real damage to another child.

The violent behavior characterized by bullying does not disappear with time. On the contrary, as bullies are rewarded for their behavior by an increase in status among their friends, a more exciting social life as they engage in illicit activities with others, release of anger or frustration and even material gain in cases of theft or mugging, they are likely to continue and intensify their activities rather than grow out of them. In many cases, bullies grow up to commit crimes, abuse drugs and alcohol and otherwise continue the destructive behavior they were never taught to avoid. Their victims continue to suffer as well, frequently undergoing depression and anxiety unless they are empowered to counteract bullying in effective ways.

Myth 3. Bullying affects only the bully and victim.

Eight-year-old Travis had always enjoyed the short walk home from the large combination elementary-middle school six blocks away. A number of kids walked home the same way, and Travis was always able to find someone to talk to. His parents were surprised, then, when a few months after school began Travis started asking to be driven to and from campus. At about the same time, he began having nightmares that left him exhausted in the mornings. When his parents questioned him about what was going on, Travis refused to talk about it. Soon, however, he started asking to stay home from school, claiming that his stomach hurt and that he thought he had the flu.

It was only after Travis's father took him to be examined by his pediatrician and the two men talked with Travis seriously that the boy confessed to having witnessed a terrible incident on the way home from school. It seemed that while Travis was walking home with a new boy named Philip, several bigger boys had cornered them and demanded their backpacks. Travis had run away, but when he looked back he saw that the boys had grabbed Philip and, when he resisted, hit him several times and pushed him down into a ditch. Travis, too frightened to defend his friend or get help, went home and said nothing. The next day Philip was absent from school. In fact he never returned. Travis had heard rumors that the older boys had "gotten Philip," but he would never learn what happened to him.

Travis's nightmares dated from that experience. Even though Philip's tormentors had not threatened him afterwards, Travis lived in fear that they would try to silence him. Though nothing had happened to him directly, school no longer seemed safe to him, and the six-block walk home from school was a daily nightmare. In addition, he experienced terrible guilt for not having helped his classmate. He felt, vaguely, that he deserved to be punished for what he had not done.

Unless an incident directly involves their son or daughter, many parents tend to ignore the presence of bullying behavior in their communities and schools. Educators sometimes contribute to this silence by refusing to discuss such incidents out of concern that they will negatively affect the school's reputation. Yet a number of studies have demonstrated that bullying not only affects those directly involved in the conflict but also negatively impacts the sense of safety and general satisfaction of all students in the school.

Certainly, the recently publicized mass shootings at schools have increased the level of anxiety among many students who were not directly involved. According to a 1999 poll conducted by ABC News and the *Washington Post*, four in ten high school students believe they have classmates who feel troubled enough to carry out a Columbine High School–style massacre. One in five of those surveyed claim to know a fellow student who has brought a gun to school, yet 83 percent say they did not report this fact to an adult. Such awareness necessarily distracts students from their academic activities and causes them to wonder whether they will be the next victims of an assault.

Students do not need to brandish weapons to create anxiety throughout a school. Dan Olweus's studies of anti-bullying programs in Norway, and a number of studies in the United States as well, have demonstrated that even ordinary bullying measurably decreases school morale and academic performance, while effective anti-bullying programs lead to improvement in these areas. Much as in our larger society, everyone is dragged down when violence is allowed to take place on school campuses. Effective policing and education turn our schools and communities into safe havens where our children can thrive.

WHO GETS INVOLVED

Myths exist not only about the role that bullying plays in childhood and adolescence but also about the types of children who are likely to become bullies or victims and the reasons behind their behavior. Such misconceptions prevent us from recognizing certain actions as bullying and from responding in productive ways.

Myth 1. Only boys are bullies.

Marta lived with her two children in an inner-city neighborhood with a public high school ill-equipped to handle incidents of bullying or violence. Marta frequently saw groups of boys from the high school hanging out on the corner near her apartment, lording it over the younger kids and, as far as Marta could tell, looking for trouble. Though Marta wished her older daughter, Amy, did not have to deal with this situation, she could not afford to send her daughter to private school or move to a different neighborhood. Instead, she prepared Amy for her first year of high school with plenty of warnings about how to avoid the wrong kind of attention from "bad boys" and whom to talk to at school if she needed help.

To Marta's relief, Amy didn't seem to be bothered much by the boys on the corner. A good student who soon became active in extracurricular activities, Amy spent her time with kids who did not use intimidation or violence to gain attention. Amy's school experience was, for the most part, very happy through the first half of her freshman year. She had won a part in the school play and was off at rehearsals so often her mother hardly ever saw her. Suddenly, though, at around the time the play was performed, Amy started spending more time in her room. Marta noticed that she looked haggard and anxious. There were just as many phone calls for her as usual, but Amy went out less now, preferring to cruise the Internet rather than go out with girlfriends.

"Are you okay, honey?" Marta finally asked her daughter. "You've been looking pretty sad lately." Amy shrugged and, after a silence, admitted, "Some of the girls are teasing me." Marta relaxed. "Oh, that's all," she said. "Well, girls like to tease. You can take care of yourself, though, right?"

Amy didn't answer, but Marta assumed that her daughter would be fine. The school year ended, summer passed, and another school year began. This year, however, Amy seemed to have changed utterly from the confident, high-performing student she had been before. She spent a lot of time away from home, but not, as far as Marta could tell, involved in school activities. The telephone rang for her much less often. And the spark that had once been so prevalent in her personality seemed to have disappeared.

Around midyear, Marta got a telephone call from the school's counselor. The woman asked Marta to come in to discuss Amy's "situation" regarding some of the other girls in her class. When Marta met with her, the counselor explained that half a dozen girls had been suspended for using classroom computers to "flame" unpopular girls—Amy included. The flames, or insults, passed along via e-mail and Web sites referred to Amy as a whore, included lists of boys with whom Amy had supposedly had sex, and provided made-up quotes from boys about how Amy performed in bed.

Stunned, Marta confronted her daughter that night at home. "It's true," Amy told her, crying. "It started when I got the lead in the play last year, and Sandra Sullivan didn't. Her boyfriend said I deserved it because I read better, and Sandra let me have it. She got all her friends to gang up on me. They've been writing stuff about me on the bathroom walls. They follow me around school yelling insults. And they have all this stuff on the Web. It's terrible, Mom. I've even thought about killing myself just to end it."

Once Marta understood how deeply her daughter had been affected by the cruelty of the girls at school, she was able to get help for her daughter and support the school counselor's efforts to stop the bullies' behavior. However, a great deal of damage had already been done. A year of Amy's high school career had been destroyed, and she would always wonder whether her fellow students remembered and believed the rumors that had been spread about her. "If only I had listened last year when Amy talked about the teasing," Marta told the counselor at one point. "I could have saved her so much pain. But all I could think about were the boys in the neighborhood and protecting her from them."

Many parents make the same error in judgment that Marta made in this situation. It is an easy error to commit, since statistics show that boys are more likely than girls to engage in bullying activity, particularly when it comes to physical violence. Yet girls can be bullies, too, even if they never raise a hand to their victims. Female bullies commonly act by spreading rumors, teasing, ostracizing and otherwise causing emotional torment. It is vital, therefore, for parents to educate their sons and daughters about how damaging such behavior can be to others and not to discount a child's complaint just because the damage isn't physical.

Myth 2. Bullies are social outcasts.

Brent was well known in his community as a kid who had everything. His father was a successful attorney who owned one of the largest homes in town, and his mother spent much of her time volunteering. Brent's two older brothers had dominated their senior classes before going off to college. Like them, Brent was well dressed, well groomed and good-looking. He had plenty of friends.

That was why it was so difficult for Jane Matthews, the vice principal at the local high school, to believe Sam, a tenth-grader, when he told her that Brent had beaten him up behind the soccer fields after school. True, Sam's clothes were torn and he had a huge black eye. But Sam was a scruffy boy from a poor neighborhood who tended to hang around the edges of crowds without being invited in. Jane knew Sam because he had been sent to the office a number of times for skipping school and earning poor grades. She couldn't imagine why Brent would bother with someone like him.

Comparing the two boys' backgrounds, Jane came to the conclusion that, for some reason or other, Sam was lying or mistaken about the identity of his attacker. But as the year passed and a few more reports about Brent trickled in, Jane began to wonder whether she'd been mistaken about this star of the school's debate team. Only months later, when a dispute at a basketball game led to a bloody fight between Brent and a boy from the opposing school, did Jane begin to suspect that the reports about Brent were true.

Brent's fight with the boy led to a civil suit from the victim's parents, and this in turn led to professional intervention. As Jane learned too late, Brent's family had a history of problems dealing with their feelings of anger and aggression. His two older brothers had abused him throughout his early childhood, unchecked by parents who were rarely at home. As it turned out, the older boys had a reputation among their fellow students for sudden outbursts of violence. Most of Brent's "friends" admitted that they were more afraid than fond of him. Though he was able to fool adults with his manners and good looks, he was having serious problems with self-control. Now that he had reached late adolescence, his hangers-on had started to wise up to his problem and had begun to drift away.

As Brent's situation illustrates, and as a large number of studies have shown, the relationships within a family are far more powerful influences on a child's way of expressing aggression than are his socioeconomic status, racial identity or any other broad external characteristics. Bullies appear just as frequently in middle-class and wealthy communities as in poor neighborhoods, among whites as among minority groups, and in suburban as in urban settings. According to a 1994 study by Louise Bowers, Peter K. Smith and Valerie Binney of the University of Sheffield, bullies tend to have a weak relationship with their father (whether or not he is physically present in the home), experience a lack of family warmth or cohesion, and have negative relationships with siblings. The image of a bully as unpopular and disliked is also erroneous. Bullies have been shown in a number of studies to enjoy an average or above-average level of popularity, since their young classmates want to identify with a "winner" and may even be entertained by their cruel behavior. Fortunately, as children mature toward the final years of high school and begin to comprehend the moral weakness underlying such actions, bullies' popularity starts to decline.

In the meantime, however, bullies may be top students, captains of the sports teams, ace debaters or otherwise leaders among their peers. The distinguishing factor between bullies and non-bullies is not their social status but their inability to channel or control aggressive feelings—and this inability can show up in anyone.

Myth 3. Kids who get picked on are "weaklings" or "nerds."

Tom and Martin, both nine years old, had lived next door to each other nearly all their lives. Tom was an easygoing boy who was extremely overweight, wore thick glasses and could sometimes be obnoxiously loud. Martin had always been very smart and good-looking, though also solitary and introverted—a boy who preferred playing board games with his parents in the evenings to hanging out with kids in the neighborhood. Martin's handsome face and intelligence apparently counted for little among his peers in light of his social insecurity. As Tom's mother, Laura, a secretary at their school, often observed, Martin was picked on constantly at school, while Tom was one of the most popular boys in the class.

Asked to describe a typical victim, most adults (and children) will probably guess that such a child is overweight, wears glasses, is poorly dressed or otherwise "uncool." It is true that according to many studies, including a 1991 survey conducted by Richard Hazler and colleagues at Ohio University, junior high and high school students identify a victim as someone who does not fit in, has a different religion, wears unique or unusual clothes, has a physical weakness or is different in appearance. However, while these qualities may render a child more vulnerable to the *possibility* of bullying, they do not guarantee that it will happen. In order for bullying to occur, other factors—such as poor social connections and poor social and/or academic support systems at school, and the low self-esteem they tend to foster—almost always come into play.

If Tom had been left on his own at school, his unusual looks may have caused him to be singled out for bullying. But his mother's experience with elementary school children had helped her prepare her child for this possibility. From his earliest childhood, she had taught her son specific ways to deflect hostility with humor, to attract friends and create a base of social support, and to look to teachers and other adults for help when necessary. As a school employee, she was able to monitor his experience to some degree. She had occasionally spoken to teachers about the possibility of his being taunted or abused, and she knew that her actions had heightened their awareness of his situation.

Laura was fond of Martin, too, and was troubled to see that his parents appeared unaware of his problems at school or at least had done nothing to intervene. She feared that if Martin received no help, his tormentors would feel free to intensify their bullying—perhaps even leading to Martin's abusing other children as a way to escape his position. When Martin came down with the flu, Laura came up with a plan. She arranged for Tom (who had already had the virus) to bring Martin his homework. Over math homework—and video games—the two established an unlikely friendship. By the time Martin returned to the classroom, he had an ally who could begin to bridge the social gap between him and the rest of the class. And Tom had an interesting, creative new friend.

FIGHT OR FLIGHT? HOW TO RESPOND

Some of the most damaging myths on which parents, educators and other adults rely have to do with the best ways for children and teens to respond to physical, verbal or social abuse from their peers. By handing out common but ineffective advice, adults send children into a truly dangerous situation unarmed and unprepared. No parent would allow a toddler to use scissors without keeping a close eye on him, and few would consider letting a child ride a bike or a skateboard without a helmet. Yet every day parents send their children and adolescents onto the school-yard battlefield with no protection from abuse.

By considering some of the following misconceptions about how to deal with bullies, you may be better prepared to advise your own child as he struggles to manage similar situations. With plenty of adult support and guidance, children can learn how to discourage violent behavior among their peers—making attending school a safer and more enjoyable experience.

Myth 1. Ignore a bully and he'll leave you alone.

When twelve-year-old Stephanie reported to her social studies teacher that a boy in the class kept taunting her, the teacher advised her to ignore him. "Harry probably just has a crush on you," she explained to the girl. "That's how boys are." In fact, Harry had asked Stephanie to go to the movies with him a few weeks before and Stephanie had turned him down. She had told Harry that her parents didn't let her date yet, which was true—but it was also true that she disliked the boy. She had heard that his father had died the previous year and his family was having problems, but she still didn't want to spend time with him.

After having talked with her teacher, Stephanie decided to follow her advice and try to ignore Harry's taunts. But ignoring Harry just seemed to goad him further. One day he followed Stephanie down the hall after class, screaming insults at her. Though Stephanie was crying by the time they reached the end of the hall, she refused to respond to her attacker. As they reached the top of the stairs, the boy gave her a hard shove, causing her to fall to the landing below.

As Stephanie's teacher should have realized, ignoring a bully is no solution to the problem of harassment. Bullies are motivated by a need for power, a need to control, and an inability to direct their aggressive feelings in more acceptable ways. As many studies have demonstrated, ignoring their behavior usually leads to an *increase* in violence.

Since an overwhelming amount of bullying takes place at school, teachers' attitudes toward aggression play a large role in its prevalence. By ignoring the behavior of Stephanie's attacker, her teacher seemed to tacitly condone it. Bullying will only begin to decrease when educators, parents and students agree to stop treating it as an acceptable form of behavior.

Myth 2. Stand up to a bully and he'll go away.

When ten-year-old Clayton began coming home with a new bruise or cut nearly every week, his mother, Rita, wanted to talk to his attacker and his parents. Her husband, however, believed that

Clayton needed to take care of the situation himself. "If he just hits back once the guy will go away for good," he insisted. To prepare for the face-off, Clayton and his father spent a weekend practice-fighting. Clayton had never been physically aggressive, but by Sunday evening his father felt he was capable of at least a short fight. The opportunity came a couple of days later when Clayton was cornered on the playground by the bigger boys who had tormented him all year. As soon as their attack began, Clayton threw a punch. Five minutes later, he was left bleeding and bruised on the tarmac for a teacher to find, the victim of the worst beating he'd ever received.

When advising a child to "just fight back" in order to discourage a bully, it's important to remember that bullies always choose victims who are weaker, younger, smaller or less powerful than themselves in some way. This relative strength does not have to be physical: while an older child may use his fists against a young victim, a small, quick-witted child can bully, too, by taunting or ridiculing his larger victims—and a socially adept bully may successfully isolate a shy classmate no matter how strong she is. Chances are that if your child has been tormented regularly by this bully, he will not win an outright fight with him in the arena the bully has chosen (physical fighting, taunting or social manipulation). Obviously, defeating the victim rarely discourages abuse; rather, it provides positive reinforcement for the abuser and encourages him to continue. Instead of giving your child lessons in encouraging violence, consider showing him how to enlist adults' help and to avoid situations and settings that lead to bullying. Meanwhile, make sure that the places where your child is bullied (the playground, the school bus, the classroom) are well patrolled, and inform the adults in charge of your child's care about the bullying. You can also talk with the bullies' parents about the situation and make yourself available to help protect your child in every way that you can. Once bullying episodes turn violent, it is paramount that they be stopped before they escalate.

Myth 3. Bullies never change their behavior, so it's up to the victim to solve the problem.

Twelve-year-old Sherry and her family had only recently moved to a big northern city from the rural South, and she was looking forward to starting junior high school in a completely new world. However, from the very first day, Sherry got the message that she did not fit in. The socially dominant girls in her grade were quick to target her for taunts, social isolation and practical jokes. They called Sherry a cracker who was too ugly to look at and too dumb to live. As she told her mother, "My clothes are wrong, my accent's wrong, even the music I like is wrong. My life's a joke, Mom. I want to go back home."

Sherry's mother, Alma, responded by trying to help her daughter conform more closely to her classmates' culture. She bought Sherry a dozen new outfits, helped her work on her accent and enrolled her in an after-school dance class that some of the more popular girls attended. By the end of the year Sherry had indeed managed to blend in with the crowd. But Alma found that she liked her less. Like her former tormentors, Sherry now made fun of other girls who were not in her clique. Her grades had dropped and she seemed to have few interests. When Alma asked what had happened to the Sherry she used to know, her daughter told her, "This is the me who can survive here, Mom. You do what you gotta do."

Both Alma and Sherry suffered from the misapprehension that bullying indicates a fault with the victim and that it is solely the victim's responsibility to correct the situation. There was nothing wrong with providing her child with a few new outfits to help her fit in, but Alma should also have addressed the bullies' behavior by speaking with Sherry's teachers and, if possible, the bullies' parents.

The girls at Sherry's school could have benefited in the long run from guidance on how to tolerate others' differences, and Sherry would have been better off if she had known that such bullying is never acceptable and that her unique personality was worth preserving. If that had been the case, she might not have turned to bullying others as a way to solve her problems.

THE TROUBLE WITH MYTHS

Facing a bully is a terrible experience that no child forgets. Facing a bully without parental support or other supervision almost certainly leads to an increase in suffering and, in the long run, despair. When adults choose to ignore bullying behavior or hide behind the convenient myths of their culture, they leave their children vulnerable to whatever dangers come their way. To protect our children we must alert ourselves to the signs of trouble, listen carefully to what they tell us and act in rational ways to help them resolve the situation and move to safer ground.

In the following chapters, I will explore the types of bullying that nearly every child witnesses at one point or another in her life. I will describe ways to empower your child to respond productively in such situations, to address this issue yourself and to persuade educators and other professionals to come to your child's aid. The first step, however, in helping any child—bully or victim—is to recognize the warning signs that indicate something is wrong, to ask the right questions and to pay close attention to how the child responds. We *can* act to combat bullying wherever we find it. But in order to act, we must listen and clearly observe.

CHAPTER THREE

BULLYING: WHO, WHAT, WHEN, WHERE

"I'm not going to school!"

"Don't be ridiculous, Jeff. Get your shoes on."

"I'm not going!"

"Why on earth not?"

"I don't wanna. I don't like it."

"What don't you like?"

"Laurie. She teases me. She calls me stupid."

What parent hasn't experienced some variation on this type of discussion—an exchange that leaves so much room for interpretation it's difficult to know how to respond. Is Laurie really the reason this child doesn't want to go to school? Is she really teasing him? Only once, a few times, or every day? Are her attacks a case of deliberate bullying or is she just trying to get this child's attention—perhaps even flirting with him in a childlike way? Should adults intervene? Should Jeff be encouraged to go back to school and face down his tormentor? Is this the only case of bullying he is subject to, or a mild example of more widespread taunting and other types of abuse?

In the previous chapter, we discussed how and why to avoid responding to such statements with, "Nonsense. Just ignore her and she'll leave you alone." We explored the dangers of making assumptions about a child's experience based on stereotypes and myths. But if you now know how *not* to respond to your child's reports about bullying, how *do* you respond instead? Given children's limited ability to express themselves and reluctance to report negative experiences to their parents, how can you form a picture of what is really going on?

The first step must be to expand your understanding of bullying beyond the limited assumptions discussed in Chapter 2. You need to know just how likely it is that your child is being bullied or is bullying others, as well as where, when and in what form abuse tends to occur. In later chapters I will discuss ways to encourage your child to share his experiences with you. First, however, it's necessary to prepare yourself to better handle such news by considering the typical realities of a child's life.

IS *THIS* BULLYING?

Frank had complained before to his parents about the older kids down the street. "They call me 'doofus,' " the seven-year-old reported. "They say they're going to get me someday when you're not looking. They follow me to school and call me names."

Maybe it was the silly sound of the word *doofus*, or maybe it was the children's young age (Frank's tormentors were nine), but Frank's parents were reluctant to take any action against the older kids. They reassured Frank that the boys were "just teasing" and tried to keep an eye out for them when they were out of the house. But since Frank stopped mentioning the incidents, and only words had been used, they soon forgot about the problem—that is, until the day that the boys carried out their threat. Frank's parents got a call from the school informing them that Frank had been found crying in a bathroom stall, his shirt torn and his head bleeding. His attackers had stolen his lunch money, smashed his head into the bathroom sink, and told him they would kill him if he told anyone who had hurt him.

As Frank's parents learned, taunts, insults and other seemingly mild forms of abusive behavior can not only hurt a great deal but, if ignored, may lead to even more damaging acts. Children who become the object of teasing and name-calling may eventually face total ostracism. Bullies who verbally threaten their victims may decide to carry out their threats. Teenagers subjected to gossip may begin to face sexual harassment, cruel practical jokes and other forms of abuse. For this reason, it is important to take *every* form of abuse seriously—to consider whether the attack was deliberate, whether it was repeated and whether the aggressor was aware that she was hurting her victim—and to help your child respond in an appropriate way.

Physical Abuse

Jay is a seventh-grader, very bright and quick-witted. He has a great sense of humor and always makes his mom and older sister laugh. Even after his dad died a few years ago, it was Jay who seemed able to get everyone to smile and go on. Since the school year began, though, Jay's mother has become worried about him. "He's just not his happy old self," she says. She has noticed that twice in the last two weeks Jay has come home with torn clothing, and his favorite jacket is missing. When she asks him about these things, he is evasive and seems upset.

One day the school principal calls to say that Jay has been in a fight with an eighth-grade boy and that he is being suspended for two days. Jay's mom goes to school and sits with Jay and the principal while Jay, sobbing, tells the story of the past two months.

Three boys a year older than Jay ride the bus to school with him each day. From the time Jay gets on the bus and walks back to his seat until he arrives at school thirty minutes later, these boys sit next to him, punch him on his upper arms and torso, call him a wimp and demand that he turn over his bag lunch. Being in the back of the bus, they are out of sight of the driver. While other students witness this intimidation daily, most are seventh-graders themselves and are afraid to speak up or even move. When a girl told the boys to stop one day, they turned to her and began to hit her as well.

By the time Jay gets off the bus at school he is bruised, lunchless and on the verge of tears. The boys have warned him that if he tells anyone about their little "fun" on the bus, they will break his arm. Jay believes them. The bus ride home is often the same. Jay prays that the boys have an after-school activity so he can ride in peace. Some days he runs into one or more of them in the bathroom. Usually, they sidle up to him and give him a little punch to remind him that they are in control. On one occasion, they trapped him in a toilet stall and wouldn't let him leave until he was late to class. As he ran to join his classmates, concerned about how he would explain his tardiness, one of the bullies punched him hard in the stomach and he fell to the floor. When he returned to class, hunched over in pain, he told his teacher he was having stomach cramps.

Now, telling the story, Jay is crying—not only from the pain he has been enduring but from fear that the bullies will come after him. He lifts his shirt to reveal dark bruises on his arms and chest. Some are new, but many look as though they have been healing for a while. Jay feels frightened, helpless and hopeless. His mother starts to cry at the sight of his wounds and the thought of what he has been going through.

When most parents think of bullying, images of physical abuse come to mind. Of all forms of cruelty, physical bullying can certainly be easiest to identify and is most likely to spur adults to action. While less common than verbal abuse (taunts, insults, teasing and gossip), physical attacks happen often enough. Children are kicked, punched, pushed and otherwise abused on the playground, on the school bus, on the way home from school and within their own homes. Thousands of violent incidents are documented in our schools each year. According to the National School Safety Center's

Report, *School-Associated Violent Deaths*, 269 students and school personnel died in violent incidents on or near school grounds in the eight years prior to 2000.

Hitting, shoving, kicking and other forms of physical abuse are most common among boys (both as bullies and victims), but can be experienced by girls as well. Among boys, physical bullying becomes more common during junior high school and begins to decrease during the final years of high school. Of course, a great deal of hitting, biting and other types of physical acting-out takes place in early childhood, when physical expression of all kinds is the norm. This is not considered true bullying, since only after around age four or five do children begin to understand that hitting or biting causes pain. Still, even before age five, physical acting-out behavior should meet consistently with correction ("We do not hit people. If you are mad at Andrew, I will help you tell him how you feel"). If you find that your toddler or kindergartner is being subjected to repeated abuse, you are right to insist that caregivers or teachers protect your child, while teaching the aggressor better means of expression.

Elementary school children are quite likely to meet with physical abuse, both from their peers and from older kids. (Some schools have attempted to address this by housing their kindergarten through third-grade classrooms in a building or wing separate from older grades.) Many such incidents are the result of unpremeditated outbursts of anger. Others—repeated attacks, deliberate violence, abuse that continues long after the victim has protested and the attacker knows she is causing harm—are examples of bullying behavior that must be stopped.

As children grow larger and stronger in adolescence and have more access to weapons, physical violence becomes increasingly threatening—even as it begins to decline in frequency in the later high school years. Gang violence becomes more of an issue along with other forms of off-campus ambushing and group attack.

Teenaged boys occasionally abuse girlfriends. (According to a recent study on domestic violence, many high school boys think it is all right for a boy to strike his girlfriend if she angers him.) Older teenagers deliberately harm younger children. As adolescents grow less willing to share their personal lives with their parents and other adults, it becomes more difficult to monitor this type of behavior and help a teenaged victim. In Chapters 4 and 5, I will discuss some clues to look for in determining whether violence is a major element in your child's life.

Verbal Abuse

When Matthew was three years old, he was attacked by a neighbor's dog while playing outside his house and suffered damage to his face. Although most of the damage was corrected surgically over the next two years, Matthew's right ear remained slightly misshapen. His parents were relieved that the lasting effects of the accident were so minor. For Matt, however, his ear was a problem. Since first grade, his classmates teased him mercilessly about his "stupid ear." They called him earless, earboy, ugly and retardo. At first when this happened, he was quite upset. He would come home from school crying and saying he was dumb and hated school. His parents told him to ignore what the kids were saying. But ignoring them didn't decrease the teasing. Matt started to wear a hat to cover his ears, but that made him stand out all the more.

Now, in fourth grade, Matt claims he is used to the teasing. Most of his friends are understanding and know he's sensitive about the subject. But whenever Matt meets new people, he feels anxious and afraid that he will be the subject of continued verbal abuse. He often appears sad and, although he is happy with his family, he always seems defensive and cautious around his friends.

Taunts, name-calling, threats and gossip—all forms of verbal abuse—are the most common form of bullying, yet they are the least likely to be taken seriously by adults. While boys tend toward physical bullying in early childhood, they indulge in an enormous amount of taunting, name-calling and threatening during the late-elementary and junior high years. Girls, who are typically more verbal, often begin using words as weapons at a younger age and remain partial to this type of bullying throughout their school years. In fact, verbal abuse is so integral to the culture of middle childhood that children frequently fail to recognize it as unusual or cruel. This may be one reason why girls are less likely than boys to be described as bullies.

Name-calling and teasing begin early among children, but they become true bullying only as children begin to wield them deliberately and become aware of how hurtful words can be. Preschoolers' and early elementary school children's natural fascination with language soon leads to an awareness that "naughty" words grab others' attention. Along with her classmates, your child is likely to graduate from the ever-popular "poo-poo head" taunts of four-year-olds (when the "bad" word may well delight both speaker and recipient) to the somewhat more deliberate "slowpoke" and "dummy" of second or third grade. Occasionally, a sexual term is picked up from older kids or parents and passed around, though at this age few children understand the meaning of such terms. In most cases, verbal taunts and name-calling during this period are not really bullying, since the "attacker" is not fully aware that she is hurting someone. Still, it is vital to respond to name-calling and threats with consistent disapproval even when the words are innocently used. A child needn't be blamed for her actions at this age, but she must be taught that verbal abuse is not acceptable behavior.

During middle childhood (roughly fourth grade through junior high), children become much more aware of words' power to hurt others. Many children this age become obsessed with lobbing put-downs at both friends and enemies. Words such as *turd*, *retard* and *lard-butt* are used as boot-camp-style bonding tools (particularly among boys) as well as weapons. While boys tend to prefer name-calling, taunts and threats, girls frequently use negative labels and rumor-spreading to ostracize a fellow student and assert their own power. This practice is hard on younger children, who are so frequently the defenseless victims, but it can also cause lasting damage to the self-esteem of those entering the fragile emotional state of adolescence. Certainly, few adults have forgotten the names they were called, the gossip spread about them or the threats they received from their classmates, neighbors and others during this time.

Because kids aged nine to fourteen are generally well aware of how damaging their words can be, their actions constitute true bullying. It is important for adults to work with the child to change her behavior and make sure that abuse meets with appropriate consequences. (I will suggest a number of ways to do this in Chapter 7.) Don't forget, too, that the victim also needs attention. In Chapters 4 and 7 I will provide you with ways to listen effectively to a child who is being verbally bullied and help her deal with this very painful experience.

By late adolescence (about age fourteen to eighteen), the fascination with generic name-calling begins to fade, but is sometimes replaced by experimentation with racial, cultural or religious slurs and sex-related name-calling. Teenagers continue to use verbal bullying to bond with others (gossiping about a classmate), seek revenge ("flaming" an enemy or rival) or establish dominance (taunting a less aggressive child). By now, their actions are fully deliberate and they should suffer the consequences.

Fortunately, during the final year or two of high school, many teenagers begin to grow more idealistic and supportive of others. Those who continue to bully others find that their popularity declines. A number of sixteen- to eighteen-year-olds can be persuaded not only to condemn bullying in others but to defend those who are being victimized.

Whatever age your child is when you learn that she is being verbally abused or is being cruel to others, resist the tendency to ignore the situation because it's "only words." Not only do words frequently lead to other types of abuse, as I have mentioned, but they are extremely damaging to young children in and of themselves. As I have seen time and again in my own practice, the results of chronic verbal bullying are a sharp decrease in trust, lowered self-esteem, depression and anxiety. Many children resort to violence against themselves or others solely in reaction to this type of abuse. Your child needs and deserves your guidance in such situations, and her attackers need to be stopped.

Social Abuse

Fifteen-year-old Sally is a thin, attractive and wholesome-looking young woman. She has mild acne and stoops slightly when she walks, almost as though she's trying to go unnoticed. During the past summer, Sally moved with her family to a small town from a big city where she was well accepted but not the most popular girl in the school. She hadn't made any friends near her new home by the time school started.

Sally liked some of the girls she met early in the year and was hoping they would accept her. Despite her tentative attempts to make contact with some of these girls, they did not seem to take to her. Sally's mom told her that they might have felt threatened by the fact that she was smart and beautiful. Like most adolescent girls, Sally didn't believe she was either. It was clear to her, however, that the girls in this small school were different from what she was used to. She was worried, but she had a plan.

Sally would try out as a JV cheerleader. She was athletic enough, and after working out with the squad, she just knew the other kids would start to like her. So she went to tryouts after school. When she walked into the gym, she saw a group of three of the most popular girls standing together. One looked up and said to Sally, "What are you doing here, girl? We don't allow lesbians to be cheerleaders." Another girl chimed in, "You think you're better than us, but you aren't, you're just a slut from up north." They turned their backs on her and resumed their conversation.

Sally made the JV cheerleading squad. The sponsor liked her. She worked out with these girls and a few others for nearly a month. Every time she went to practice or boarded the bus, they turned up their noses and moved away, muttering insults. Sometimes they would talk openly about parties or upcoming social events, knowing that she could hear them. When they did address her directly, it was to deliberately exclude her. "Are you coming to the party at Pat's this weekend? Oh, I forgot, you're not invited!" Sally was talking to a boy in the hall after school one day when one of the girls came up to them and said to the boy, "You don't want to go out with her, Christopher. Everyone knows she'll sleep with anything that moves." After a month, though she loved to cheer, Sally couldn't take it anymore and quit.

The boy no one will sit next to in the lunchroom. The girl no one greets in the halls at school. The teenager whose phone never rings and who never goes to parties. These are, frequently, the victims of social abuse, and if you don't believe this type of ostracism causes deep and lasting pain, you have forgotten how it feels to be a child or adolescent. Social abuse—deliberate shunning, rejection, ostracism and cruel practical jokes—grows increasingly common as children grow older, reaching its apex in early adolescence. Possibly because its effectiveness depends on the subtle balance of power between one child and another—a social consideration in which girls frequently show more interest—it is more prevalent among girls than boys. A girl whose best friend hangs out with her in private but ridicules her to others is being socially abused. A boy who finds mud, insects or worse slipped into his lunch box every day is being bullied socially as well.

As with verbal bullying, the seeds of social abuse begin in early childhood, when young children's expanding social awareness leads them to experiment with boundaries ("No boys allowed!"). This is an age when children frequently reject one another in tactless ways ("He's too fat. I don't like him.") and enjoy the feeling of power they get from either excluding or accepting new additions to their group.

Much of this behavior is normal and even necessary at this age. Children learn to define themselves in part by defining what they are *not* (not a boy, not fat, not the new kid). Learning how to exclude others in acceptable ways takes time and effort, and children this age cannot be expected to follow such social rules every time. Still, as with verbal abuse, this is the time to begin teaching your child how to *appropriately* avoid another child. The key lies in understanding a young child's limitations and working consistently to teach him social skills.

By middle childhood, girls in particular become more sophisticated in their understanding of the ways of exclusion. This is a time of very painful ostracism, when being perceived or perceiving oneself as "different" can destroy a child's emotional well-being. At this age, children should certainly be aware that deliberate shunning or targeting causes pain and is therefore bullying. In milder cases—when a child causes suffering by turning away from a former friend—it may be possible to talk with the aggressor and help her find less damaging ways to break off the friendship. In more extreme instances—when children deliberately bait their victim and stage a public humiliation—adults must respond immediately and make it clear that such behavior will not be tolerated anywhere. In many cases, of course, bullies have their reasons for abusing others in this way. They may have been socially victimized themselves or may have learned such behavior at home. Nevertheless, such cruelty is unacceptable, and all adults involved must focus on communicating this message.

By late adolescence, social bullying begins to decrease somewhat, though "revenge"-based exclusion, often involving boyfriend/girlfriend situations, becomes more popular. The social abuse that does occur can be more damaging than in earlier years, since teenagers are able to invent more effective ways to humiliate others and have more freedom to do so. (The classic horror movie *Carrie* offers an excellent example of social bullying at this age.) Such chronic or ex-

__*CULTURAL BULLYING*__

As children move from childhood into adolescence and encounter a host of new social situations and related emotions, some respond to such social anxiety by bullying those they perceive as "different." Sadly, in many cases the "different" children are those who belong to a minority culture, race or religion with which the bully is unfamiliar. Particularly in cases when the victim is alone, without the support of others like himself, cultural bullying can become a source of great torment. If teachers and other school officials belong to the bully's cultural group, the victim may not feel safe turning to them and may instead act out his anger and fear by fighting back or picking on younger children. It is not surprising that children who have been bullied in this way, through absolutely no fault of their own, sometimes end up by late adolescence in worse trouble for aggressive behavior than their original abusers.

Since a basic unfamiliarity with the rituals and behavior of the victim's culture is often at the root of a bully's behavior, it is important to begin educating your child about the lives other people lead from early childhood on. Taking advantage of cultural events and programs that involve children of many ethnicities or religions will introduce your child to others' viewpoints and perhaps allow him to make friends with individuals from other groups so he can learn how much he and they have in common. Keep an eye, too, on news events that feature certain ethnic groups or cultures, since these are sometimes used as an excuse by teenagers to target particular children who happen to belong to that group. When such an event occurs, ask your child whether any kids at school may belong to that culture, ask him how he thinks they might feel as negative comments about their group are publicized, and talk about ways for your child to make sure another person's experience is not made worse by ignorant taunts and gossip.

treme instances of cruelty lead many teenagers to thoughts of suicide or other forms of violence. Certainly, they can negatively affect
academic performance, school attendance and self-esteem. In
Chapter 4, I will discuss ways to learn whether your child is suffering from social bullying and, if so, how to help her respond effectively.

Sexual Abuse

*Tanya, an eighth-grader in a large urban junior high school, has many
girlfriends and hangs out with them after school. Since school started, she
has become more interested in boys and they have started to pay attention to
her. She is a bit shy, though, and while her friends are able to describe their
encounters with young men, she has little to contribute. Still, she is excited
about learning more about interacting with members of the opposite sex.
Her interest has been recently heightened by the school dance that will take
place in a few weeks.*

*About a week before the dance, Will, a boy in Tanya's class, approaches
her while she is at her locker. She doesn't know Will at all except to see him
in the halls at school. Will is very large for his age, handsome, powerful
and intimidating at the same time. He stands close to her (a little too close,
she thinks) and says, "I'll see you at the dance." Tanya is not sure if that is
a question or a statement. She nods, just to get him to go away.*

*The following day, as Tanya is walking to class, Will comes up to her
again and says under his breath that he will see her next Friday and they
will have some "fun." Tanya's girlfriends don't hear the remark but do say
that Will is really cute. Tanya feels creepy about her interaction with Will
and a little frightened. Given what her friends have said, however, she
doesn't want to share her feelings.*

*When the day of the dance arrives Tanya is excited, but worried
about Will. He hasn't said anything else to her, but she has noticed him
staring at her more than once. She really wants to have fun at the dance
with her friends and not be worried. About an hour into the dance, Will*

comes over to where Tanya is standing with her friends. He asks if she will come out into the hall with him for a minute. She looks to her friends for guidance and they smile and nod, indicating that she should go.

Once in the hall, Will encourages Tanya to walk around the corner with him. He stands very close to her and pushes her gently up against the lockers with his body. He reaches into his pocket and takes out a condom in an unopened wrapper. He shows it to her and says, "Want to put this on me?" He presses his pelvis against her and places his other hand on her breast, rubbing it through her blouse. Tanya is feeling panicky. She doesn't know what to do. She pushes Will away and runs back to the dance. He walks slowly behind her saying, "Aw, c'mon, just you an' me, baby."

Once back with her friends, Tanya tries to stay calm and act as though nothing has happened. Throughout the next week, Will will come up to her in the hall and stand close to her, touching her on the arm and on her rear end and whispering, "Next time, Tanya."

While sexual abuse between adult and child has received a great deal of attention over the past decades, the frequent occurrence of inappropriate touching, sexual labeling ("slut," "faggot"), intimidation and rumor-spreading among peers has largely escaped adult attention. As a result, many parents are unaware of the extent of sexual abuse among teenagers and the fact that it also takes place in middle childhood and sometimes even earlier. According to a 1997 study, one in five high school girls reports having been physically or sexually abused, with nearly one in ten of the older girls reporting abuse by a date or boyfriend. The real numbers are probably much higher, since sexual assaults are among the most underreported crimes, and teenagers are even less likely than most to report them. A 1993 study by the American Association of University Women reports, for example, that 80 percent of all American students have been sexually harassed (when harassment is defined as including sexual abuse, gestures, dirty jokes and even glances) and 76 percent of all boys.

Sexual harassment of boys is perhaps the least likely form of bullying to be reported or addressed. Yet it occurs quite frequently, leaving severe emotional and sometimes physical damage in its wake. Adult men sometimes recall abuse during childhood from teachers or other adults, as well as peers. Homosexuals in particular—both male and female—attract abuse as bullies find their sexual difference so threatening. Nearly every adult homosexual can recall an instance of humiliation and pain at the hands of peers at just the age when they were first exploring their emerging sexuality and were most vulnerable to abuse.

If your child is courageous enough to confide in you about an instance of sexual abuse, take her account seriously. Even if you believe the aggressor is acting out of ignorance rather than malice, be sure to let your child know—through actions as well as words—that such behavior is not acceptable. As teenagers grow, they need to be taught the social rules for flirting, dating and other sex-related social activity. They need to know about boundaries (asking a girl out is okay; grabbing her breasts is not), respect (talking about another person's sexual activities is cruel and therefore unacceptable) and the ground rules for courtship and romance (harmless flirting makes both parties feel good; sexual harassment is one-sided and leaves the other person feeling bad).

Sexual abuse cuts to the core of a child's or adolescent's developing self-image. No one, no matter how young or old, deserves to be ignored or left unprotected from such cruel harassment.

WHO BECOMES A BULLY

"Every hour of seventh grade was a nightmare," Robert, now a successful photographer, recalls. "There was one guy who just decided he hated me—I have no idea why. I had never even noticed him before. He turned all of his friends against me and they made my life completely miserable. They'd come up behind me and shove me, they slit the tires on my bike, and after I fixed the tires they stole the bike. But over the summer between seventh and eighth grades, I started doing weight training and had a huge growth spurt. When I came back to school in the fall I was bigger and stronger than the kid who'd been bothering me. That seemed to do the trick, because he and his friends never bothered me again. I didn't have to do anything about it."

It is hard to comprehend, for both parent and child, why anyone would deliberately and systematically torture a classmate. The fact that a bully can take practically any form makes the situation even more confusing. Your child may be tormented by the stereotypical tough-talking boy from a broken home, by the "well-behaved" girl who spreads cruel rumors about him or by a sibling when his parents are out. Some bullies earn bad grades in school and have problems with alcohol. Others are popular members of the football team who are on the honor roll. (Such bullies may try to maintain their popularity by focusing their aggression on children who are weak, unpopular, and unwilling or unable to retaliate.) Family wealth or status seems to have little effect on whether a child becomes a bully; abusive behavior occurs in children rich and poor. Many children can be kind and friendly on their own, but behave like bullies in a group.

Clearly, something deeper than economic disadvantage or lack of popularity is at work when a child feels compelled to abuse others. To better understand these causes, British researchers and authors Peter Stephenson and David Smith have subdivided bullies into *dominating bullies*, *anxious bullies* and *bully-victims*. Dominating and anxious bullies, the researchers found in a study conducted in 1989, frequently come from homes in which power issues dominate and in which sibling interaction is more powerful than child-parent relationships. Parents who rarely talk as equals with their children and expect their demands to be met without question, for example, might encourage bullying behavior in a child. A child who gets into the habit of dominating a sibling and whose parents fail to intervene may also grow up assuming that physical, verbal, social or sexual abuse are both effective and normal. It is easy to imagine a wide variety of "types" who might fit into this category: the child of a dominating parent who punishes frequently and praises rarely; the privileged girl whose parents rarely make an effort to curb her aggressive behavior; the teenager in a poor household whose parents are too overworked to supervise their many children. While all of these are stereotypes, their number and variety illustrate how impossible it is to judge a bully by outward appearance alone.

Bully-victims are children who have been victimized themselves, by peers or adults, and whose pain and frustration have led them to escape their situation by bullying others. In many cases, they also come from households where they are rarely supervised, parenting and discipline are inconsistent, and parental warmth is low or absent—in other words, where they received little or no adult help when they themselves were victimized. A number of studies have shown that the most common response to victimization is anger. Without adult help in channeling their anger in positive ways (getting their abusers to stop, expressing their feelings through words or positive actions), bully-victims rid themselves of the horrible sense of victimization by picking on other children. Bully-victims are considered the most potentially violent type of bully—the type to reach for a weapon or join a gang—because their rage is extremely high and their support systems very weak. In other words, they are angry, in pain and all alone.

Male bullies outnumber females at a ratio of about five to four. Studies have described male bullies as dominating, disruptive in class, unable to concentrate and behaving in a "tough" manner. Female bullies have been described as talkative, rude, dominating and using bad language. However, the family dynamics I have described run deeper than gender or surface behavior. It is important not to discount your child's report that he is being bullied just because the aggressor is physically smaller than your own child, is well-behaved with adults or is a girl. Before you laugh at the possibility that the head cheerleader is torturing your child, find out as much as possible about the attacker—from her teachers, her parents and other adults as well as her peers. You may uncover clues that will help you begin to understand the problem behind the impulse and, as we will see in later chapters, address the problem more effectively. Keep in mind, too, that the forces that operate in a typical bully are not magically resolved upon graduation from high school. Many children are bullied by the adults in their world—teachers, coaches, parents and other relatives. There is no reason to exclude anyone from consideration. Bullies are defined by the behavior they exhibit, not their age, size, appearance, status or bank account.

FACTS ABOUT BULLIES

Bullies have been defined by author and psychologist David Elkind as "children who consistently try to control peers through verbal or physical aggression to relieve their own feelings of inadequacy." A bully, as opposed to a child who is generally aggressive, is likely to:

- target only those children who are perceived to be weaker in some way
- be unwilling to accept others' ideas
- be unwilling to negotiate during play
- often oppress or harass others in either a physical or mental way
- be of average or above-average popularity

WHO BECOMES A VICTIM

Peter, a child of one of my colleagues, was big for his age. In second grade, he was several inches taller than any of the other boys in his class and looked like a fifth-grader. Yet he came home from school frequently crying because, he said, the other kids were picking on him. My colleague found this hard to believe, since none of the other children stood as tall as Peter's shoulder. Yet a talk with Peter's teacher led her to understand that it was true. It was difficult to get Peter to explain the dynamics of what was happening with the other kids, since he was only seven, but as it turned out he was afraid to defend himself against the bullies because he was afraid he would hurt them. Conscious of his large size, Peter had become a victim out of kindness. My colleague, who had confessed to dark thoughts about a "loser" son, felt properly rueful and began dealing with Peter's confusion about how to respond.

We all carry images in our heads of the stereotypical "victim." We may imagine a small boy with big glasses, a girl in unfashionable clothes or a child from another race or culture. The same traits also exist in nonvictims, however. Again, Stephenson and Smith have found that the reasons why certain children become victims run deeper than gender, appearance or race. In their 1989 study, they classified victims as *provocative victims* and *passive victims*. Provocative victims seem to actively draw bullying responses to them through repeatedly pestering, baiting, insulting, invading another child's personal space and so on. Some such children may not yet have learned correct social behavior. Many others' acts are a consequence of ADHD (attention deficit/hyperactivity disorder), oppositional defiant disorder, Tourette's syndrome, dysemia or any other conditions that involve an inability to recognize social boundaries or other aspects of accepted behavior. Victim-bullies, who act out their anger through physical means and frequently meet with retaliation, also fall into this category.

Classical victims are frequently shy, anxious or afraid. They generally possess some form of weakness, or *perceived* weakness, in relation to the bully. They may be physically smaller, of lower social rank, poorer or unwilling to fight back—but it is their shyness, anxiety or fear more than any of these traits that renders them victims. An unattractive girl may avoid being bullied, in other words, if she has a healthy self-image and good social skills. A boy from a minority culture may escape persecution if self-confident wit makes him popular among his peers. Even a smaller boy can evade abuse from his larger classmates if he gets the support he needs to relieve his anxiety and build his self-esteem in other areas.

As you can see, children become victims for so many reasons that it is foolish and destructive to make stereotyped assumptions about any child's experience. Some victims need only a bit of instruction in social skills to remedy their situation. Others need emotional support, confidence-building and the protection of concerned adults. A few may need medical or psychological intervention to help them avoid inadvertently provoking aggression in others. By looking past the stereotypes to the root causes of victimlike behavior, you will be in a much better position to help your child.

WHERE AND WHEN IT HAPPENS

"I can barely remember one happy day from my childhood," an adult client told me. "My big brother tortured me from birth, I guess—at least from before I learned to talk. He hardly ever picked on me in front of our parents, but they both had jobs and were out of the house a lot. My brother was expected to babysit, and that was when he would start. He'd scare me to death with ghost stories, tell lies—like my parents were going to sell me to buy dog food—throw

---

FACTS ABOUT VICTIMS

Victims may be defined as those who continue to be exposed to aggression from others over time. A victim is likely to:

- be shy, fearful and/or anxious
- have low self-esteem
- be socially isolated
- be physically weak
- be emotional (if male)

---

me against the wall when I got on his nerves, and lock me in the closet for hours with no lights on. My parents never believed me when I tried to tell them how he was. I couldn't wait to get out of that house."

This unfortunate woman's parents may have been very effective in protecting her from bullying in the neighborhood, but they had clearly never considered their own home a possible setting for abuse. While it is true that most bullying takes place on school grounds in unsupervised locations such as the playground, school bathrooms and locker rooms, practically any poorly supervised place is eventually used. The school bus and bus stop are likely locations for daily torment, as is the walking or bicycling route to and from school. Bullying can take place on any street corner, vacant lot or empty field. Even public swimming pools are not exempt. Recently, several girls in New York City reported being grabbed and having their swimsuits hiked up or off while trying to cool off in the sweltering summer heat. A great deal of social, verbal and other types of abuse occurs in classrooms with a teacher present (roughly half of teenaged students report that teachers try to stop bullying only "once in a while" or "almost never") and at home among siblings or abusive adults.

Most psychologists will tell you that summer camp remains one of the prime sites where bullying occurs and continues relatively unchecked. Perhaps because of the intense atmosphere created by large numbers of children cooped up together with insufficient supervision, summer camp lends itself to escalations of hostility and deliberate cruelty. Before you send your child off to camp or any other longer-term adventure, consider the possibil-

CYBERBULLYING

As children and teenagers become more comfortable on the Internet, bullying has established a growing presence on-line. Recently, a number of parents in New York City were stunned to discover their children listed in an on-line poll as among the city private schools' "150 biggest ho's." In the nearby suburb of Chappaqua, a Web site run by two male high school seniors listed the phone numbers, addresses, family histories and supposed sexual experience of approximately forty girls. In Dallas, a graduate of a suburban high school relentlessly harassed a sophomore girl at the school on a message board thread entitled "Lauren is a fat cow moo bitch."

Most on-line bullies are protected by the First Amendment from criminal prosecution. The Dallas sophomore, who was also insulted on-line for her weight and the fact that she had multiple sclerosis (the message board included the words "Die bitch queen!" repeated for more than a page), was able to defend herself through official channels only after the harassment moved offscreen. After her car was egged, insults were written on the sidewalk outside her house and a bottle full of acid was tossed at her mother as she opened her front door, a report was filed with the Dallas Police Department.

ity of verbal, physical or even sexual abuse and refer to these chapters for ways to talk with your child ahead of time about how to deal with it effectively. Assure your child (without scaring him) that the lines of communication will remain open even when he is away from home, and that if he has any serious problems, you will be there to help him.

TEACHING YOUR CHILD TO RECOGNIZE BULLYING

By now, you are probably more aware of when, where and among what types of children bullying is likely to occur. It is just as important for your child to recognize when bullying is taking place and how to differentiate it from "just kidding around." When discussing such behavior, ask her the same questions I suggested you consider in Chapter 1:

- Did the child hurt you on purpose?
- Did she do it more than once?
- Did she make you feel bad or angry?
- Did she know that she was hurting you?
- Is she more powerful than you in some way?
- Did you hurt her first?

If your child protests that her attacker can't be a bully because she's president of the seventh grade or the most popular girl in class, talk to her about what you've learned about bullies and their identities. If she is not sure whether a particular act is a case of bullying or a flubbed attempt to be friendly, encourage her to get a reality check from others who were present, talk with an open-minded teacher or other adult and discuss the experience with you. Meanwhile, use your knowledge about where and how bullying may occur to see that your child's environment is properly supervised. Young children who suspect that they may be ambushed by bullies should not be left to walk home alone. Teenagers subject to sexual harassment should not attend parties with no adults present. Recognizing a bully when she sees one is a valuable tool for any child, but if your child is left unprotected, recognition is not enough.

CHAPTER FOUR

IS MY CHILD A VICTIM?

"School starts tomorrow. Are you excited?" Deborah Newman, a child psychologist in Boston, asked her seven-year-old, Alex, as she tucked him into bed. "What do you wish most to happen in second grade?"

"I wanna do good in spelling," her son told her.

"Uh-huh."

"I wanna learn more math."

"Okay."

"And I want the big kids to leave me alone."

Dr. Newman stopped tucking in the sheet. "What kids?"

"The big boys in fifth grade." Alex's voice sounded small and scared in his dimly lit room. "They beat me up all the time last year. I hope they stop."

Dr. Newman was stunned. As she gently prodded her son for more information about the bullying he had experienced the previous year, she asked herself how, as a professional therapist, she could have missed the signs that her young son was being abused. Yet it can be quite difficult, even for adults experienced in working with children, to know when problems occur. Younger children may be unable to clearly communicate to their parents what has happened to them, or it may simply not have occurred to them that this is something adults should know. Older children and teenagers who are being bullied frequently feel too ashamed, or too fearful of parental interference, to say anything. Many children's first instinct is to try to handle such situations themselves rather than risk being called a snitch by their peers or, even worse, punished by the bullies themselves. Past experiences with unresponsive adults may discourage a child from talking about new problems. Research has shown that even children who have not had a negative experience with a parent or teacher may perceive adults as ineffective because so many adults are present in school and yet bullying occurs there all the time.

Yet it is vital to your child's health and well-being to address any bullying situations as quickly as possible. Obviously, any child who is being physically or sexually abused risks permanent injury. Children who are being harassed or feel unsafe for any reason are likely to experience difficulty sleeping, nightmares, intense emotional states (fear, anger and depression), stress-caused illnesses (stomachaches, rashes) and other problems that impact their health. Their preoccupation with the abusive situation leaves them unable to concentrate. The result is often a drop in grades and social activity, which leads in turn to a drop in self-esteem. Though many parents consider the extreme reactions to bullying—suicide or an outburst of violence—rare and unlikely in their child's case, a survey by the British organization Kidscape revealed that more than 20 percent of bullying victims reported at least one attempt to kill themselves. Certainly, we all hope to learn about and resolve bullying incidents long before the children in our lives reach that desperate state.

We can do so by being alert for signs of abuse and taking the all-important first step of determining just what's going on when we do see them. Children are often unable or unwilling to confide in adults about being victimized, so you'll need to know what to look for in determining whether your child is being victimized. When the signs are clear you'll want to learn all you can about the situation, and the primary source will be your child. You must learn how to talk with your child or teenager in ways that will enable him to communicate his problems to you, and to respond to what can be shocking information in ways that encourage him to trust you. Unless you ascertain the facts first, your efforts to resolve serious conflicts may go awry.

COULD MY CHILD BE A TARGET?

In Chapter 2, I addressed the common belief that kids who get picked on are almost always "different" from nonvictimized children in some way—that is, they are overweight, unusually dressed or members of a minority race or religion. I also pointed out that, while such characteristics may increase a child's chances of being harassed, they do not make harassment inevitable. Many a child dressed in off-brand jeans and sneakers manages to avoid abuse, while others who appear perfectly ordinary suffer teasing, ostracism, name-calling and worse.

When trying to determine whether *your* child may be a victim, it is important to look beyond surface appearances to the real elements that determine which child a bully will target. The essential quality that any bully looks for in a victim is not difference but *vulnerability*—some indication that the bully can abuse this child without retaliation. If your child wears less fashionable clothes but has good social skills that provide her with plenty of friends, she is not particularly vulnerable to attack. (Her friends will help defend her against a bully.) If she is somewhat isolated and not adept at social interaction she *is* vulnerable, regardless of her race, religion, socioeconomic status or physical appearance. Studies have shown that the following additional characteristics, all of which signal vulnerability to a bully, are the most likely to lead to a child's victimization:

- physical weakness
- small stature
- shyness
- low self-esteem or lack of confidence
- lack of family communication and support
- unwillingness to respond aggressively to aggressive behavior
- anxious or fearful response to bullying
- poor self-control or other difficulty with social skills
- possession of material items that a bully might want

In reviewing this long list, it is easy to see that the children bullies choose to pick on are those least likely to fight back. A *passive victim* may attract abuse because she is emotionally sensitive (responding with obvious fear and anxiety when harassed and thus rewarding bullies for their efforts), comes from a close, protective family (where she has not learned to cope with aggressive behavior) or wears nice clothes (making bullies believe she may have something worth stealing). Shyness, a lack of friends and absence of adult support will make her an especially likely target. Low self-esteem may cause her to endure abuse long after other children would find ways to resist. Continued bullying will only decrease her self-esteem further, leading to more bullying in a continuous cycle until and unless adults intervene.

The types of social or behavioral difficulties experienced by many children with ADHD and most behavior disorders lead to victimization in another way. These children, termed *provocative victims* by researchers, unintentionally annoy their peers and as a result are more likely to be abused by them. Children from cultures whose social norms are different from those of the majority may also fall into this category and find themselves the brunt of abuse for reasons they (and often their parents) cannot understand.

While it is difficult for any parent to see his or her child in an objective light—especially as that child appears to her peers—assessing your child's personal style and social skills is a vital first step in protecting her from bullies. If you are unsure whether her personal style tends to isolate her at school, talk with her teachers or school counselor about their impressions of how well she functions socially compared to others her age. Ask other parents who know your child to provide you with a reality check about your child's behavior and social experience—and listen carefully, because you may share the same traits, and it is particularly hard to recognize social stumbling blocks that we experience ourselves. To gain a better personal perspective, schedule or participate in group activities that include your child—soccer practice, Scout meetings, get-togethers of schoolmates in your home—that will enable you to directly observe her in a social context. As you watch, keep in mind that you are not trying to learn whether she is behaving "correctly" or not, but whether she is acting in ways that make her *vulnerable to abuse*. A child who refuses to respond aggressively when bullied clearly understands that lashing out at others is bad (and should be praised for her self-control), but she needs to learn other ways to respond that will actively discourage more bullying in the future. In Chapter 7, I will describe many such effective responses and other methods and attitudes your child can adopt to become less vulnerable. For now, it is important to focus on identifying any aspect of your child's behavior—no matter how well meaning and laudable in other ways—that endangers her safety outside of her home.

HOW WILL I KNOW
THAT SOMETHING'S WRONG?

Most parents do their best to keep the lines of communication open with their children. Yet even the most attentive adults will not learn about everything that's going on in a child's life. If your child is being victimized, chances are quite good that he will never tell you about it. To protect him, then, you will have to take an active role in observing his behavior, talking with him in ways that encourage him to discuss his problems, and demonstrating your ability to help him stop the bullying quickly and permanently so that he can get on with his life.

The following warning signs may indicate that your child is being victimized at school, at home, in the neighborhood or elsewhere:

- Acts reluctant to go to school
- Complains of feeling sick; frequently visits the school nurse's office
- Shows a sudden drop in grades
- Comes home hungry (because bullies have stolen his lunch money)
- Frequently arrives home with clothing or possessions destroyed or missing
- Experiences nightmares, bedwetting, difficulty sleeping
- Acts afraid of meeting new people, trying new things or exploring new places
- Refuses to leave the house
- Waits to get home to use the bathroom
- Acts nervous when another child approaches
- Shows increased anger or resentment with no obvious cause

- Makes remarks about feeling lonely
- Has difficulty making friends
- Acts reluctant to defend himself when teased or
  criticized by others
- Shows a dramatic change in style of dressing
- Has physical marks—bruises, cuts, etc.—which may
  have been inflicted by others or by himself

If your child exhibits any of these symptoms, he needs your help—and he needs it now. You can best assist him if you know precisely what has been going on. Ask his teacher, school bus driver and other adults who spend time with your child—as well as any sympathetic classmates of his whom you may know—whether they have noticed any incidents involving him. Is he taunted on the school bus? Does he sit alone in the lunchroom or on the playground during recess? Has he tried to talk to any adults about being harassed, or have others been disciplined for harassing him? Listen carefully to what these people have to tell you, but do not assume that nothing is wrong if they say they have noticed nothing. A 1999 study conducted in several Midwestern schools by Dorothy Espelage of the University of Illinois indicated that while teachers accurately identified 50 percent of bullies, they were able to pick out only 10 percent of their victims. The victims' classmates were even less accurate in identifying which children suffered abuse. All too frequently, a victim suffers anonymously while everyone—adult and child alike—focuses on the abuser.

While you are questioning those who spend time with your child about his experience, keep in mind the effect your questions or remarks may have on their future relationship with your child. It is terribly painful for a child to be repeatedly victimized, but the pain is intensified when well-meaning adults or children embarrass, isolate or otherwise single him out. Such an experience only lowers the child's self-esteem further, rendering him even more vulnerable to abuse.

To avoid this type of situation, focus on remaining in a neutral "information-gathering" mode for now. Refrain from overreacting if your child's bus driver casually mentions that yes, he's noticed that your child is "roughed up" in the back of the bus almost every day. Note a teacher's unwillingness to involve himself in your child's difficulties, but wait to address his apathy until you have all the facts. When talking about your child with one of his peers, keep the subject matter general ("Does Anthony seem to get along okay with the kids at school?") and avoiding naming any "suspects," who may hear of your suspicions and retaliate against your child.

Of course, your child is the best source of information about exactly what has been happening to him, and in the next section I will address ways to encourage him to share his experiences with you. In the meantime, though, consider other ways to help your child through this situation without unduly embarrassing him, and otherwise approach his personal life with sensitivity and tact.

IS SHE BEING SEXUALLY ABUSED?

Most children who are bullied tend to keep their problems to themselves, but children who are sexually abused are particularly likely to avoid confiding in adults. Sexual abuse causes acute feelings of shame, guilt and embarrassment in its victims. Children are likely to feel that they are somehow to blame. In her book *Slut! Growing Up Female with a Bad Reputation*, author Leora Tanenbaum describes a sexually labeled teenager's experience this way: "She is publicly humiliated in the classroom and cafeteria. Her body is considered public property. She is fair game for physical harassment. There is little the targeted girl can do to stop the behavior. I was surprised to learn that teachers, generally speaking, do not intervene; they consider this behavior normal for teenagers."

(continued)

Tanenbaum goes on to point out that sexually active girls are not the only ones who are labeled with such words as *slut* or *whore*. Any girl who demonstrates vulnerability—especially sexual vulnerability—may be harassed in this way. Girls who mature physically before their classmates, wear the wrong clothes or have been sexually victimized through date-rape or other such scenarios are all likely victims of sexual bullying.

In addition to the warning signs for all types of bullying listed above, victims of sexual abuse may exhibit any or all of the following behaviors:

- withdrawal from family, friends and/or normal activities
- excessive bathing or poor hygiene
- regression to younger, more babyish behavior
- eating disorders such as bulimia or anorexia
- passive or overly pleasing behavior
- sexual activity or pregnancy at an early age.

All bullying violates children's feelings of self-confidence and control, but for obvious reasons sexual abuse can lead to the most extreme emotional responses. When trying to discern whether your child has been sexually labeled, taunted or abused, take *extra care* to protect her privacy and help her maintain her self-esteem.

HOW CAN I TALK WITH MY CHILD ABOUT BULLYING?

"So, David, how are things at school these days?"

"Umm . . . okay."

"I never heard how that field trip to the newspaper offices went. Was it interesting?"

"Mmm."

"How's your friend Sean these days? He hasn't been over here in a while."

"Can I go now, Dad? I've got homework to do."

If you have recently had a conversation like this with your child, you may doubt my assertion that all children, no matter what their age or situation, want their parents to know how they are and would love to be able to rely on them in times of trouble. Yet, as I have learned through many years of treating abused children (and as most of us will realize if we look back on our own childhood and adolescence), this is truly the case. In fact, lack of adult interest or involvement in their experience is what leads many victimized children and teenagers to turn to such drastic remedies as suicide and other forms of violence.

Yet your child may have very good reasons for withholding information from you. As I pointed out earlier, she may feel shame, guilt or embarrassment over the bullying experience, or even believe it is her fault that she was singled out. She may fear that you will blame or punish her if you learn what has been going on. If her attacker has threatened her or someone else with harm if she tells anyone about the abuse, her reluctance to speak up makes perfect sense.

If your child is still quite young, she may be incapable of communicating her experience to an extent difficult for most adults to understand. I am reminded of one woman whose son had complained of intense headaches nearly every weekday morning during the school year, but felt fine once summer vacation began. The child's pediatrician could find no reason for the headaches and referred him to a counselor. The counselor soon learned that the boy had been victimized all of the previous school year by a group of older boys who threatened to beat up his younger brother unless he handed over his lunch money daily. Looking back, the child's mother realized that the only days her son did not have a headache were the days when she packed him a box lunch—leaving him with no lunch money. Her son was too young to be able to describe the situation to his mother in conventional ways, but his body expressed his dilemma loud and clear.

If you suspect your child is being victimized and have noted such nonverbal signals of abuse, you will still want to confirm your suspicions by talking with her about it. To open the doors of communication, you will need to speak to her in ways that are clear, simple and direct. Vague questions such as "How was your day?" are too open-ended to get results from younger children and too easy for a teenager to dodge. Specific, concrete queries are much more likely to lead to the flood of information that your child is quite likely longing to provide.

Following are some specific questions that may start you and your child on the road to a real interchange of information. You will need to adapt these questions to your child's level of sophistication and personal circumstances:

For Younger Children

- Have you been eating your lunch?
- I notice that your shirt is torn. How did that happen? Did someone do that to you?
- I notice that you haven't seemed to want to go to school these past few days. When I was your age, sometimes I didn't want to go to school because other kids used to push or tease me. Does that ever happen to you?
- Do you ever have fights at school?
- How has the ride on the bus been lately? It seems pretty crowded. Are you ever scared or bored on the bus? Would you like it better if I drove you to school?

- Sometimes I get so angry I want to hurt somebody, even though I would never do it and realize it's wrong. Do you ever feel that way?
- Has anyone ever touched you in a way you don't like? Where and how?
- Do people tease you or make fun of you because you are a boy (or girl)? What do they say?

For Older Children and Teenagers

- It seems like you haven't really wanted to go to school. Is there something going on there?
- Are there doors on the stalls in the rest rooms at school?
- Would you like to have some friends over sometime?
- Do you ever feel so mad and frustrated that you want to hit somebody?
- Who are your friends now? If we could get tickets to the ball game, who would you ask?
- Are there a lot of cliques at your school? What do you think about them?
- Do you feel like your clothes fit in at school? Do a lot of kids wear stuff like that? Like who?
- I developed early when I was a teenager and guys always used to tease me about my body. Do they do that to you?
- Has anyone ever tried to touch you in an inappropriate or sexual way without your permission?

You may be surprised at how frequently specific questions such as these lead to emotional confidences from your child. On the other hand, they may have no obvious effect as she continues to protect herself in the only way she knows how. If your questions meet with little more than stubborn silence, carefully observe your child's behavior. Does she respond by muttering a general response and turning away? Does she suddenly march upstairs to her room and shut the door? Does she look embarrassed or as though she wishes she could run away? If so, something is probably wrong, and it is up to you to demonstrate—over and over until she believes you—that confiding in you and getting your help is a better solution than living with her situation on her own.

How you gain your child's confidence depends in large part on her age. Younger children frequently respond to being read stories about other children in similar situations. You might read such a story at bedtime, when your child is likely to feel relaxed, and then gently ask her whether she has ever felt as the child in the story did. Teenagers may respond to discussions of newspaper articles about bully-related violence. Tales of your own childhood experiences are effective for children of all ages. Set an example for your child by confiding in her about the time you were victimized and how you responded. This can be an especially powerful way to connect if you and your child share a particular vulnerability—shyness, few friends, a culture that is different from that of your neighbors'. Keep in mind that in all of these instances you are working to build up your child's trust in you so that she feels it is safe to confide her troubles. Invading your child's private life by reading her diary or e-mail will have the opposite effect and should be avoided except in the most extreme instances. Even if you do manage to discover the truth of your child's situation in this way, by violating her trust you will have lost the opportunity to help her.

Once your child does begin to tell you about her experiences, try hard to respond in supportive ways no matter how shocked or frightened you are by what she tells you. Let her know you believe her, that you support her, and that together you will find a way out of this difficult situation. If you sense that she may be distorting the facts or is behaving badly herself in some way, you can address those issues later. Initially, though, it is extremely important that you solidify her trust by *listening carefully* to what she says and avoiding any judgmental comments. So many teenagers whom I have counseled—many of them in prison or mental health facilities— have insisted that they tried to confide in a teacher, parent or other adult as their feelings of depression, despair or rage grew more extreme, but that the adult either ignored or criticized them. Children, and especially teenagers, are quick to note when an adult is not interested in helping them, and victims of bullying feel especially vulnerable to judgment. Don't isolate your child even more by withholding your support.

WHEN SHE'S HIDING MORE THAN ABUSE

Parents may chafe at their children's reluctance to confide in them, but many children have very good reasons for hiding the truth of their lives from their families. As you lay the groundwork to encourage your child to talk with you about the abuse she is experiencing, you may be surprised and even shocked by the facts that start to emerge about her life, especially if they concern sexual activity or identity. You may learn that your daughter or son is routinely called a *slut* or an *ice queen,* a *fag* or a *lesbian* at school or on the Internet. You may hear frightening rumors that have been passed around about her—rumors that may turn out to be true. Your child may confide in you that she does indeed have sexual relations, is being sexually abused, has a sexually transmitted disease, is pregnant or is gay.

(continued)

Before you begin trying to talk with your child about her personal life, then, it is a good idea to prepare for any difficult news you may receive. Think about how you will respond to information about sexual activity. What kind of response do you think would best help your child? What counseling and other resources are available to help her and to help you support her in her efforts to improve her situation? Who is better at handling this type of situation—you, your child's other parent, or another relative or adult friend? Are all of the adults involved in her care generally in agreement on how such situations should be addressed, or do you need to discuss these issues and come up with an approach that's acceptable to all?

Of course, you may find that your greatest concerns are unfounded and that your child simply needs your help with a specific social situation. Still, it's best to think through a variety of possible scenarios in advance so that you are not caught off guard at the critical moment when your child confesses the truth of her situation and observes your response. If you believe you may not be able to act supportively no matter what she tells you, consider offering her an appointment with a professional counselor instead. There are cases when it's better to let a child take her problem to an outside expert than risk family conflicts that only make the situation worse.

Every child suffering harassment or abuse needs adult support. It is vital to ask questions and otherwise involve yourself in your child's life, no matter how much you sometimes wish you didn't have to hear about the problems she has encountered. Above all, be patient with your child and don't give up. Children's fears and resistance can be great, but in most cases they hope their parents will win this contest of wills. Chronic bullying is a profoundly alienating experience that can lead to suicide or extreme violence against others. Sadly, most parents ask the necessary questions far too late.

CHAPTER FIVE

IS MY CHILD A BULLY?

THERE ARE FEW EXPERIENCES a parent dreads more than getting a phone call from a school official or other parent reporting his child's bad behavior. The feelings of shame, embarrassment and even resentment are perhaps most intense when the bad behavior involves cruelty to another child. *How could he have done that?* you are likely to ask. *It isn't possible. My child isn't a mean person. Why would he deliberately hurt someone else?*

Before you deny that your child could possibly have been involved in a bullying incident, however, consider the fact that bullying in some form occurs quite frequently every day, at school, in the neighborhood and anywhere else children congregate. Even if your child did not instigate the action, he may have contributed to it by failing to intervene when he saw another child being beaten, spreading rumors that others invented, or reading and forwarding on-line slurs instead of deleting them or telling an adult. It can be hard for a child to avoid contributing to many types of cruelty, since many children consider this the only way to make themselves socially acceptable or to keep from being bullied themselves.

If your child is one of the many who have engaged in this type of activity, understand that it is not the end of the world. In fact, the phone call from the school or another parent may turn out to be one of the best things that happens to you and your child. Research has shown that bullying most often occurs among children who are not being supervised sufficiently at home (leaving them vulnerable to picking up bad habits from others) and who are not consistently and effectively disciplined for their violent or cruel behavior (in other words, they have not been discouraged from bullying). In a way, children in this situation are "victims" of a certain type of neglect, even if this neglect is minor and only temporary. If a phone call—or your own observation of your child's tendency to be mean to others in certain situations—leads to conversations with him about others' feelings, specific lessons in how to resist cruel impulses or rechannel anger into more positive interactions, then his life will have changed for the better. Keep in mind that though bullies do frequently enjoy a certain status in the early and middle school years, their popularity starts to decrease sharply in their late teens. As adults they frequently find themselves disliked, dissatisfied and even in trouble with the law. By focusing on your child's social interaction and emotional experience now, you can guide your child toward a different future.

What you should not do is respond to such a "warning" by denying outright the possibility that your child is involved in bullying, or assuming that the victim's behavior was what caused the problem. Even if you know the victim and believe that his behavior often leads to his victimization (if he "asks for it" by crying or yelling when others tease him, or she wears revealing clothes that encourage boys to pester her), it's important to understand that your own child's bullying behavior is not a healthy response in any social situation and that his behavior must be changed. Be aware that your child will probably deny any wrongdoing, whether or not he is aware that the accusations against him are correct. (In cases of indirect bullying—spreading gossip, deliberately isolating a child, and so on—a child may actually be unaware or deny to himself that he has been deliberately cruel.) He does not want to get into trouble and may even feel ashamed, in some way, of what he has done. While you do not want to assume he is guilty if there's no proof, you can respond even to unclear situations with positive parenting techniques that will drive home the importance of considering others' feelings.

For now, think about how you can serve as a role model for him even when responding to this difficult situation. Do you express your anger and frustration by grabbing, shaking or hitting your child, calling him names, shaming him or otherwise treating him harshly or without respect? Then that is how he will behave to other children in turn. Or do you take the time you need to master your own feelings, then listen to his account of what happened and start to find ways to better his situation in the future? For many children, acts of bullying are a cry for adult attention. Use this opportunity to teach him something about how to interact with others, and reward him if he demonstrates through his behavior that he has understood.

WHAT TYPE OF PERSON HURTS OTHER KIDS?

"I never thought of myself as a bully," a teenager wrote recently in an Internet account, "but when I think back to junior high I realize that I was incredibly cruel to one person for more than a year without even realizing what I was doing. We were best friends in elementary school, but as time went on I started to want to hang out with other people. At first I just avoided him—though I never really explained why. Later, I started making fun of him to my other friends. He'd swear at me, or cry or try to hit me and I'd say, 'See, it's your fault, look at how you act!' I enjoyed making him cry. I'd report him to the teacher and he'd get in trouble, and I'd laugh. It made me feel powerful. He had major family problems that year—his brother got arrested—but even that didn't stop me. We drifted even further apart in the next years. Now, his grades have dropped and he's into drugs. We never talk to each other. It makes me sad. We had such great times together, but we never will again. I hope I have learned from my mistakes."

As is clear from this description, bullying is practiced by a wide variety of children other than the big-muscled, tough kids who may initially come to mind. As children grow and feel confronted by new drives and emotions they don't understand and often can't even name, they may behave in ways they recognize only in retrospect as cruel. For middle-schoolers especially, the desire for social status and prestige may be so great that they victimize others for the sake of gaining the clique's approval and attention. Among all children from elementary through high school, bullying behavior may be just an unexamined part of their active, fast-moving lives. Others participate in bullying to prevent being victimized themselves. By looking back on your own childhood, you may be able to recall situations in which you yourself acted cruelly—not out of cold deliberation but out of ignorance, expediency or even laziness. It is important to understand that *any* child may behave cruelly, and that the fact that your child has indulged in bullying behavior does not make her a bad person or a criminal. Rather, she is a growing child who needs your support, guidance and consistent, constructive discipline to develop into a thoughtful, caring adult.

Characteristics of All Bullies

Bullies come in practically all shapes, sizes and personality types—and both genders—throughout childhood. There are, however, certain characteristics that most bullies exhibit and that you can look for in your child. The central issue for all bullies is *their inability to channel their anger or frustration in acceptable ways.* (Remember, anger is not the problem. All children experience anger. The problem is how that anger is channeled and expressed.) In the on-line account above, for example, the bullying child felt restricted by a close friendship and did not know how to remedy his frustration in more positive ways. Not understanding his own emotions (a change in interests and desires that is a natural part of growing up) and not knowing how to escape the confines of the relationship (by inviting others to join their activities, getting involved in projects that did not include his friend and talking with him tactfully but honestly), he pushed him away in ways that were unintentionally cruel. When his victim responded with tears, blows and curses, he felt emotionally gratified by the drama that ensued. A vicious cycle of cruelty and reinforcing response was thus established—a difficult cycle to break.

No matter what type of bullying your child is engaged in, her behavior almost certainly stems from this basic dilemma: how to channel her emotions in ways that do not hurt others. A stereotype bully, who may be beaten up at home and so picks on smaller kids in the neighborhood, does so because she cannot otherwise express her profound feelings of anger and abandonment. A boy who sexually harasses a classmate may not know how to express his sexual feelings in more positive ways, or routinely fails at doing so. A girl who pretends to ignore or actively participates in others' bullying does not know how else to deal with her fear that she, too, will be victimized.

A child's inability to respond in better ways can be broken down into four subskills that you, as her parent, must consider. As you observe your child in her everyday routine, ask yourself the following questions:

• **Does she recognize and understand her own and others' emotions?** Has she had plenty of experience naming and talking about her own and others' feelings? Does she express her feelings through conversation, writing, art, physical activity, academic work or through some other medium? Does she notice others' emotional responses and is she able to empathize?

• **Does she recognize that emotional "triggers" often lead to her aggressive behavior?** Has she learned that when she is tired or feeling stressed she is more likely to lose control? Has she noticed that certain situations—spending more than a few hours with the same person, or sitting still for a long time—usually end badly? Is she aware that peer pressure is hard for her to resist?

• **Does she have the social skills she needs to manage her emotions in noncruel ways?** Does she know how to "use her words" instead of hitting? Has she learned how to "count to ten" when she's mad? Does she know how to "say no" tactfully rather than avoiding or lying to another person? Is she experienced at deflecting aggression with humor or logic rather than giving in to fear?

• **Does she have the ability and the option of communicating her feelings to others when she feels them getting out of hand?** Does she have adults to go to for help when she needs it, and friends with whom to share her feelings? Does she know that these people are available to her? Is she comfortable approaching them?

If your child lacks any of these skills or opportunities, she is at risk for bullying behavior. She is at even higher risk if she is familiar with and comfortable with violence or other types of cruelty—through her own personal experience or even secondhand from violent television shows, movies and video games. Physical strength, social status or other forms of power may also give her an advantage that she is unable to resist using.

Do Bullies Have Low Self-Esteem?

Many people assume that bullies behave as they do out of a deep sense of inferiority or low self-esteem. Much research has shown, however, that this is not the case. On the contrary, bullies have been shown to have better than average self-esteem and to enjoy average or better than average popularity until their later teens. It is this strength that allows them to pick on those whose self-esteem *is* lower and are thus vulnerable to abuse. In fact, bullying behavior has little to do with a child's level of confidence. Bullies behave in cruel ways because they *do not know better*. It is our job as adults to educate them.

HOW CAN I TELL IF MY CHILD IS BULLYING?

As a parent, you may find that you are usually the first to be blamed for your child's bad behavior, yet you're the last to know about it. Other adults who have observed your child's actions may fail to report them to you, assuming that you will respond belligerently or not at all. Your child will no doubt hide such behavior and its consequences from you for as long as he can—even convincing you that school punishments were undeserved or that he was blamed for behavior he merely observed.

Nevertheless, there are some common signs to look for that can help you decide whether there is reason for concern. First, consider the basic personal skills described in the previous section. Does your child have difficulty with these? (Of course, all children do at first, and those who continue to have difficulty can improve with time and practice.) If you are not sure exactly where your child stands in terms of emotional development, try observing his actual behavior at home. If you observe any of the following warning signs, take a closer look at your child's social behavior no matter how he tries to explain these symptoms away:

- general unhappiness or anger
- poor grades
- a tendency to act out physically instead of using words, often with adults as well as other children
- smoking or drinking alcohol
- reports of behavior problems at school
- destruction of property
- intimidation of younger children
- rudeness, use of bad language
- shortened attention span

As I pointed out earlier, your child will probably not engage in bullying behavior when you are around to observe it. You may not ever actually see him hit another child, even if he does so quite frequently. The indirect, manipulative, social forms of bullying are even harder for parents to see and identify. They can also be more easily denied or explained away ("I was just telling the truth!").

You can, however, identify the types of social *attitudes and behaviors* that may signal bullying in your child's everyday interactions. Start looking carefully at the way your child behaves when he is hanging out with his friends. (If you are not around your child and his friends very often, now is a good time to change that. Start driving him and his friends to school or to soccer games more frequently. Encourage him to invite friends over. You will not be able to help your child if you do not participate in his life.) When observing in this way, ask yourself: Does he try to dominate the others? Is he able to be patient and wait his turn? Is he willing to negotiate and listen to others' viewpoints in conversation? If someone asks him to stop doing something, does he stop? When others act in annoying ways, is he quick to lose his temper? Is he preoccupied with appearing invulnerable or tough? Does he constantly blame others when things go wrong? If you see that his social style tends toward dominance and he has difficulty listening to or re-specting others' views, then chances are greater that he does engage in bullying behavior when you are not present. Whether or not he has actually taken that next step, now is a good time to start teaching him more positive ways to interact.

Listening to What Others Say

Reports from other adults or your child's peers, painful as they can be for you, are a valuable source of information about any prob-lems your child is having. In most cases, such people, even when they disapprove of your child's behavior, are not out to "get him" or to judge you. (In fact, unless they are professionals they are proba-bly quite uneasy about approaching you and worried about how you will respond.) The fact that they have made the effort to talk with you about your child shows that they are concerned about him, and if you show them you're willing to listen and focus on the problem, they will probably be happy to help you solve it. As you listen to this adult's or child's report, suspend judgment of all parties—including yourself—for the moment. Feelings of shame, resentment and anger are not helpful right now. Concentrate on identifying the is-sues and thinking of ways to resolve them. Your child's behavior does not mean he is bad or evil. Usually it means that he feels frus-trated or depressed. Sometimes it means that he doesn't know how to act when other people annoy or hurt him. Remember that this conversation may lead to a major change for the better in your child's life, so thank your informant for having the courage to talk with you.

If you are concerned about your child's behavior, but no one who knows him has come forth with a report or opinion, don't be afraid to take the initiative yourself. Ask another parent or a mature child whom you trust for a reality check—making it clear that you are asking out of concern for all children involved and are not looking to punish or judge anyone. Seeking out help and cooperation in this way cannot only clarify what's really happening in your child's life but may also help garner valuable support from others in correcting, rather than just condemning, your child's behavior.

Is He a *Bully*, Or Did He Just Make a Mistake?

An interesting fact that has emerged from a number of studies of bullying is that, while boys report becoming angry more often than girls, boys generally describe their anger as lasting for just a few minutes, while girls tend to hang on to their negative feelings longer. These differences in styles may influence your response when you learn that your child has been cruel to another person. Did he flare up in anger, punch a classmate and then forget all about it? Or did he harbor a grudge and cold-bloodedly plan his revenge? You may also wonder whether the incident in question was an example of simple aggression (acting out indiscriminately against others, no matter who they are) or actual bullying (deliberately seeking out a victim who is somehow weaker than oneself). Remember that bullying occurs when a stronger or larger child attacks a weaker one. Fights between equals may be conflicts but are not actual bullying.

The fact is, since you will probably not be told the whole story, you may never know whether the behavior you do learn about represents a single instance when your child lost control or more systematic bullying—and, to a great extent, it doesn't matter. Since all of these types of behavior stem from your child's inability to channel his anger in appropriate ways, your best response will likely be the same. Your child needs focused attention and structured guidance. Later in this book, I will outline effective ways to help him learn to identify and control his negative emotions and to interact with others in more positive ways.

A PARENT'S STORY: "HE WHAT?"

"When my son was in middle school and high school he spent most of his time with two other boys in the neighborhood," writes Nancy, a mother of three. "None of the three of them were super-popular kids. They were all kind of geeky, to tell you the truth, and I think they stuck together mainly because they felt there was strength in numbers. Anyway, as time went on, my son and one of the boys, Kenny, became very close, while the third boy, Victor, was pushed more and more to the side. Victor had a number of irritating qualities—oversensitivity, defensiveness and basic selfishness being the worst of them—so I didn't really blame the other two kids for preferring each other's company. But about that time, I started getting calls from Victor's mother complaining about my son's 'attitude' and his 'cruelty' to her son.

"At first I was really put out by these phone calls. I felt like the mother was interfering in stuff that was none of her business and basically infantilizing her son. I humored her on the phone and said yes, yes, I'd talk to my son, but I have to confess that when I did talk with him I put it in terms of 'Please stop picking on Victor so his mom will get off my back.' Victor's mom became kind of a family joke to some extent, and my son and his friend never did stop their behavior. Eventually Victor's parents got divorced and he moved out of the neighborhood. I heard later that he went to college in England—as far away from his childhood home as he could get.

"I never see Victor's mom anymore and my grown son never mentions Victor. But lately I've been feeling real regret over that whole situation. I wish that instead of making light of what Victor's mother told me, and even ridiculing her, I'd used that information to talk seriously with my son. I can

(continued)

see now that he really was bullying Victor, and that that boy really suffered. If I'd talked with him about how his taunting might be causing Victor to act in exactly the ways he disliked, he might have started to think about how he could positively affect the relationship, and both those boys might be happier adults today."

WHY IS MY CHILD DOING THIS?

"When I was a kid, I lived just with my dad. I didn't have a mom," a fifteen-year-old boy told me. "We were really poor. He had a bad job and a lot of stress in his life. I was a victim of that stress. When he talked to me, it was almost always yelling, and I got hit a lot. I would take this abuse to school and turn it against others. It's kind of depressing, really. My dad couldn't fight back against the stress at his job. He took his frustration out on me because I was weaker, and I then took out my anger on kids who were weaker than me."

We all know how satisfying it feels, at least for a moment, to punch a pillow or a wall when we're angry, or to slam down the telephone receiver after an argument. Anger and frustration translate quite easily into physical violence or emotional cruelty, and the visceral satisfaction one feels from acting out in this way increases the chances that it will happen again.

The kind of anger that can lead to bullying behavior doesn't occur only in broken homes or in poor neighborhoods. It happens wherever children are left without enough support for whatever reason by parents, siblings, peers or others in their environment. Your child may be responding angrily to physical, sexual or emotional abuse that she has experienced from others. She may be acting out the stress she feels at home. She could be expressing sadness over your or her other parent's physical absence or lack of emotional involvement, or expressing anxiety at the *inconsistency* of your relationship with her. Research has demonstrated that inconsistency of discipline, with the parent's mood determining the severity of punishment, can be even more psychologically damaging to a child than physical abuse. If you believe your child has been acting aggressively, ask yourself if she is sad or angry about something and try to identify the cause. Remember, you can't correct bullying behavior until you understand the reasons behind it.

Rewards for Bad Behavior

Even when a child is frustrated, hurt or angry and acts out in regrettable ways, it is possible for adults and sometimes children to respond in a manner that can discourage continued aggression. Unfortunately, in some cases, children are instead rewarded for cruel behavior. Onlookers may laugh at the act of bullying, admire the bully's strength, pay more attention to him or even join in the abuse. The victim may lose control emotionally, cry, act afraid or respond in other gratifying or entertaining ways. An adult or older sibling may praise the child for refusing to put up with "annoying" people or not letting others push her around. She may experience a visceral thrill in dominating others or enjoy the material goods she steals. As long as bullying behavior is reinforced in these ways, the aggressor is likely to repeat and intensify her attacks. After all, this new way of releasing her negative emotions is winning admirers, getting more attention and, at least in her own mind, improving her social standing.

Ask yourself if your child is rewarded for aggressive behavior in this way. When you hear her say something unkind to another child, do her friends laugh? Does the crowd she hangs around with strike you as aggressive—willing to offer her friendship if she is willing to join in their abuse? Does an older sibling or adult encourage her to push back when she feels she's been pushed around, or to "give back double what she gets"? Does she seem to have more money or gadgets than you believe she can afford? If so, such reinforcers will have to be eliminated as much as possible and her behavior countered with more constructive responses (such as consistent attention, guidance, limit-setting and praise when appropriate from you and other adults) before it is likely to improve.

Your Child's Environment

Children learn to behave aggressively by imitating others. If your child's friends—or the people she hopes to befriend—treat others in abusive ways, she may also. Teachers, caregivers and other adults who frequently turn a blind eye to bullying allow it to escalate and draw in more children. Television shows, movies and video or computer games that appeal to your child's age group and glamorize violence may also lead to more aggressive behavior. These types of influences are particularly strong among children who are not exposed to many positive examples. If your child's school tolerates bullying (making it hard to find people who aren't either abusers or victims) or her neighborhood is unsafe (making it seem "normal" for children to be bullied out of their lunch money), make sure to balance those negative influences by spending plenty of time with conscientious people, especially you. Monitor who her friends are and, if you suspect that they are bullying, introduce her to alternative social venues such as a youth group, volunteer organization, sports team or after-school class. Ask her what the adults at her school do to combat bullying, and talk with your child about the probable effects on the school of doing nothing. Act responsibly in limiting the number and types of TV and other shows and games to which your child is exposed. At the very least, try to watch potentially violent shows along with her, and use any depictions of violence as a springboard for a conversation about why such behavior is unacceptable. No matter how discouraging you find your child's environment at times, keep in mind the fact that a parent's connection to his child is paramount, and your example and interest can go far in overpowering negative influences.

Your Parenting Style

As we have seen, children mimic the behavior they observe. It follows, then, that if you want your child to stop hitting or taunting his peers, you and his other family members must avoid such actions at home. Many parents respond to their children's bullying behavior with stricter rules and more extreme punishments, believing that only a rigid environment will save their children from worse behavior or even criminal activity down the road. While it is true that your child needs clear limits and you must enforce them consistently, you also need to demonstrate how anger can be better channeled. Instead of hitting, spanking or shouting at your child (even when you are legitimately angry), show him how to find a solution through talk, calm judgment and logical, nonviolent consequences. Your child needs to know that real communication is possible, and that he can resolve conflicts in positive ways if he tries.

Permissive parenting can also lead to bullying behavior when parents fail to establish or enforce proper limits for their child's behavior. Testing boundaries is part of every child's normal development—the process by which he learns what is acceptable behavior and what is not. If your child has no clear limits to push against, he will consider pushing farther and farther beyond the norm until some other authority figure—a school official, a policeman or a more powerful bully—makes him stop. Permissive parenting can also lead in some cases to "too much" empathy or sympathy for the misbehaving child. If you know that your tendencies run in this direction, keep in mind that a bullying child does not generally suffer from low self-esteem (unless he is an "anxious" apprentice to a stronger bully or a victim who has turned to bullying in self-defense). What most bullies need is education about how to behave, along with a clear idea of what their limits are and an understanding that those limits will be enforced.

Research has demonstrated that, for most children, the best approach is neither authoritarian nor permissive, but what psychologists call *authoritative* parenting. Authoritative parents take responsibility for their role in teaching their child how to behave and to interact with others, but they do not constantly *tell* the child what to do—rather, they strive to show the child how to make such decisions for himself. Such parents work to create a home environment characterized by warmth, positive interest, participation and involvement among family members. This involvement is mutual: that is, parents don't just expect their children to share with them; they share with their children, too. Such confidences ("I can't stand that guy. But I have to work with him. Before I go into his office I make myself count to ten") help children understand that their parents are fallible human beings, just like they are, and not all-powerful entities to be rebelled against.

Authoritative parenting also involves a certain degree of monitoring and surveillance of the child's activities and firm limits to unacceptable behavior. Parents expect to know where their child is, with whom, and (more or less) what he is doing. When the child violates the family's rules, his parents apply nonhostile, nonphysical sanctions. Consistency is key in these situations. As I pointed out earlier in this chapter, inconsistent discipline can lead directly to the type of frustration that causes abusive outbursts in children. Consistency also helps to clarify exactly what the rules are, and to allow your child a certain, well-defined degree of control. Just as a young child feels more secure knowing he can draw on the paper but not the walls, your child will feel more confident if he understands he can go out until midnight on Saturday nights, but must tell you who he's with and where he's going.

An authoritative approach to family life can be implemented in a number of ways—through discussion of behavioral issues, firm if sympathetic enforcement of limits, physical demonstrations of love and support (hugs as well as talks) and active participation in your child's life. Which of these ways works best in your family depends on your child's temperament—his personal style, his preferred way of communicating, his discipline needs. As I pointed out earlier, a child who is naturally impulsive or hotheaded will need more attention paid to steady, consistent but nonjudgmental enforcement of limits. A child who is larger, stronger, more active or naturally more dominant than most of his peers will need intensive training in how to keep from inadvertently hurting them. If your child loves to talk things through and hates just following orders, you may find that taking the time to talk helps enormously in winning his trust and cooperation. Other children find it much easier to obey rules and accept punishments when they help set them. Keep in mind the fact that just because your natural parenting style worked with your other children doesn't mean it will work with this one. It's important to observe each child individually and adjust some of your parenting methods to best suit his needs.

Fear

Fear of being victimized themselves is another reason why some children participate in abuse. These children, called anxious bullies by some researchers, may have little self-confidence and low self-esteem. They are not usually the instigators of abuse, but are willing to look the other way or gang up against a victim if it will win them the approval and protection of the ringleader. Children and teenagers who have been victims of bullying in the past are especially likely to join in abuse for this reason. If your child feels socially vulnerable for any reason (a drop in her family's social standing, the victimization of a close friend, a move to a new school) she may be tempted to protect her social rank in this way. A recent study in

---

WHAT TYPES OF PARENTING ENCOURAGE BULLYING IN CHILDREN?

Many factors help determine the way a child behaves with his peers, but the type of training he receives at home is a powerful influence. The four factors in the home environment that researchers have identified as most likely to encourage bullying behavior are*:

- lack of involvement or warmth on the part of the child's primary caretaker
- a permissive or "tolerant" attitude toward the child's abusive behavior (no clear limits set on bullying behavior in the home)
- use of physical punishment or emotional outbursts when disciplining children
- a parenting style that does not suit the child's natural temperament

* Adapted from Dan Olweus, "Bully/Victim Problems in School: Facts and Intervention," *European Journal of Psychology of Education,* 1997, vol. IX, no. 4, 495–510.

Minnesota showed that the number of bullying incidents increases when children enter a new, larger school, but then plateaus as children adjust to the transition.

Temperament

It is also possible (though less likely) that your child simply has an impulsive or violent personality or temperament—a natural tendency to "act out" that she has not yet learned to regulate. Such a child may experience a stronger need than most of her peers for power and dominance. Some children—especially those with a more active, physical or even verbal temperament than their peers—may be perceived as bullies and so begin to meet such expectations. Difference in temperament among siblings is one reason why, to many parents' bewilderment, parenting techniques that work with one of their children don't work with another. An older child may have naturally been slow to anger and less in need of strict, consistent limits. A younger one may need special attention if she is to learn other ways to behave.

If you find yourself frequently saying resignedly to yourself and others, "That's just the way she is," your child may indeed have been born with tendencies that can lead to overaggressive behavior. But temperament is never a life sentence. You can help your child rechannel her natural impulses and show her how to manage her greater energy, verbal dexterity or physical size. Again, becoming aware of the problem—and helping your child to recognize and monitor her own tendencies—is the first important step in working toward more positive social interaction.

HOW CAN I TALK WITH MY CHILD ABOUT WHAT HAPPENED?

If you are sure that your child has engaged in bullying, a fair, non-corporal punishment must come (see below). But it is equally important to *talk* with your child about the underlying issues that lead to bullying and *listen* to his beliefs about how social interaction works and how he can best have his way. Somewhere along the way, your child has picked up damaging lessons in how to get along with others. He has imitated the wrong kinds of behavior, found the wrong ways to express his negative feelings, or lacked the courage and support needed to withstand peer pressure. It is vital for you, as his parent, to spend the time necessary to ferret out which of these errors is responsible for his behavior and to correct his misunderstandings as clearly and supportively as you can.

This will not happen if you start your conversation by venting your anger over your child's behavior. Yelling at him, calling him names, sending him to his room without discussing the issue in productive ways, will certainly lead to more bullying in the future. In fact, because he may not regret his actions and at the same time wants you to know as little as possible about them, it may be pointless to discuss any specific incident at first. Instead, wait for an opportunity when his guard is down—over dinner, at bedtime, or when you are driving somewhere together—and talk to him in nonconfrontational ways about his experience with the issues listed in the section above.

If your child is quite young, you might start by telling or reading a story in which a child is victimized, asking him how he feels about the issues that the story brings up. You might ask, for example, "Who do you think is most like you in this story?" or "How do you think Holly felt when Jimmy called her a stupid dodo? What could Holly have done?" With an older child, you might tell a story about someone at work—a co-worker who's pretty "nerdy," perhaps, and whom most of the people at work treat without respect. You might talk about how you feel sorry for the guy, but you don't really want others to think you're good friends with him. Ask your child for advice ("What would you do if you were me?") and listen carefully to what he says. Focusing on your own dilemma may allow him to share quite a lot about his situation.

Open-ended questions can also lead to surprisingly interesting conversations once you have established a certain level of trust with your child—once he realizes that you are not going to pounce as soon as he mentions an incident in his past but are willing to suspend judgment and simply listen. Following are some questions you might try as you attempt to learn more about your child's perceptions and actions:

For Younger Children

- What do you do when you get angry at someone?
- Do you think there are a lot of weird kids in your school?

- Do you have friends who don't stand up for themselves?
- Do you feel like you need to protect yourself against other kids?
- Do you think the other kids respect you? Why?

For Older Children and Teenagers

- Why do so many kids get mugged in this neighborhood?
- Is that weird, what I did, or does stuff like that happen to you?
- Do you feel like you're stronger than a lot of other kids at your school?
- Do you feel like other kids ask you to come on to them sexually? What do you do when that happens?
- Do you think girls (or boys) really like to be teased?

However you decide to talk with your child (and you should take care to tailor your conversation to his particular interests and personal style), don't try to fit all of your questions into one conversation. Keep these talks short but relatively frequent. Vary your approach and topic. Don't be afraid to use some humor or, especially, to laugh at yourself. And take your time. If you see your child resisting, back off for the time being. It is more important to plant the seed for his own thinking than for you to try to dominate him with your beliefs.

If your child continues to be unresponsive and his behavior does not improve, he may need another responsible adult to talk to. There is nothing wrong with this, and you can best meet your responsibility as his parent by helping him find such a person. A trusted uncle or aunt, a school counselor, a pastor or rabbi or a professional therapist may be the "friend in need" who will alter your child's perceptions and belief in positive, fundamental ways.

SOCIAL EDUCATION AND EMOTIONAL SUPPORT

For most children involved in abusive relationships, talking about the issues may not be enough. A child who abuses others may need to be *taught* to recognize and respond appropriately to his own emotions, to empathize with others and to respect their viewpoints and differences, and to express himself in positive, nonviolent ways. He needs to learn how to interact with members of the opposite sex without harassing them. He must be taught how to win friends without compromising his own sense of right and wrong and how to respond to a bullying situation without being victimized himself. He must be allowed to practice his skills in environments that support positive behavior—even if you must take him out of his school, neighborhood or home temporarily to have that experience. If he is not able to learn these subtleties, he may need additional treatment or psychotherapy (see Chapter 10).

Helping your child to learn better ways to interact with others will take time, effort and a great deal of thought on your part as well as your child's. This is the price of being a parent, but it will pay off in terms of a better relationship with your child and a much better prognosis for his future. In Chapter 7, you and your child will find specific techniques aimed at helping him control his aggressive impulses. First, however, make a point of conveying to him two extremely important messages: First, that in this family bullying is never acceptable. Second, that you care what happens to him enough to become involved in his life. Even if he is resistant to your efforts at first, in the long run he will be grateful for your willingness to help him through this difficult period and even repair the damage he has caused.

CHAPTER SIX

WHEN YOUR CHILD IS A BYSTANDER

ELEVEN-YEAR-OLD ERIC had always been an active boy and was physically larger than most of the other boys his age. On one occasion he threw his considerable strength into a playground wrestling match, accidentally injuring another boy. Though the damage was minor and the other boy accepted his apology, Eric felt awful about it. A few weeks later, while a group of kids were playing football during recess, another sixth-grader shoved a younger boy hard, causing him to hurt his shoulder. When the victim reported the incident to a teacher and she spoke to the guilty boy, he claimed that Eric had done the shoving. The teacher had no trouble believing this, since Eric was much larger than the boy the victim had accused. The teacher told Eric she was going to speak to the principal.

That night at dinner, Eric's mother, Susan, noticed that her son was hardly eating anything. She asked him if something was wrong. He told her what had happened and said he was very worried about talking to the principal tomorrow.

Susan believed her son because he did not habitually hide much from her and because she knew he did not deliberately hurt others.

She prodded him for more details. Had anyone else seen the incident who could corroborate his story? Eric told her that two boys had witnessed it—one of them Gene, a good friend of Eric's.

After dinner, Susan called Gene's parents, with Eric sitting nearby. When Gene's mother answered the phone, Susan asked her to ask Gene whether he had witnessed an incident during the football game that day. Gene's mother did so, and Susan could hear Gene in the background on the other end of the line describing the incident exactly as Eric had said it happened.

When Gene finished talking, his mother said to Susan, "Are you calling because Eric got blamed for this?"

"Yes," Susan said. "We were hoping that Gene could go with Eric to the principal's office tomorrow and explain what happened. Eric's very upset about being blamed for something he didn't do, and it would really help to have some backup."

"I'm sorry," Gene's mother said curtly, "I can't allow that. Gene really had nothing to do with this and it isn't any of his business. He just saw it. I don't want him to risk getting in trouble at school. In fact, I'd appreciate it if you would not tell anyone that he witnessed this."

Susan was stunned. Didn't Gene and his mother feel any responsibility toward Eric, who could be unfairly punished? Didn't they want the person who had deliberately hurt a younger child—a boy who, according to both Eric and Gene, really was a bully—to be stopped? Gene's mother responded to Susan's objections with a variety of excuses ("Gene's not comfortable talking to the principal"; "He may just be telling us what Eric told him"), but it was clear to Susan that the real reason behind her refusal to cooperate was her fear for her child's well-being.

What a shame, thought Susan as she hung up the phone. Not only would Eric have a more difficult time tomorrow because of his friend's refusal to intercede, but the bullying would probably con-

tinue as the perpetrator enjoyed the experience of physically dominating and injuring another child without reprimand. Meanwhile,
Eric would find it difficult to forgive Gene for failing to stand up for
him, and Gene would certainly regret the rift in their friendship
that would probably follow. In fact, as Susan observed, that was just
what happened during the months that followed. Eric, shocked at
Gene's and Gene's mother's response, never really trusted Gene
again. By the end of the school year, the two boys hardly spoke to
each other. Meanwhile, as Eric reported angrily to his mother, the
bully who had not been stopped continued to push the younger kids
around and was beginning to provoke boys and girls in his own class
as well.

WHY IS IT IMPORTANT FOR
MY CHILD TO ACT?

Virtually every parent, and every child, admires the behavior typi-
fied by the good Samaritan—the willingness to step in and help a
person in need even in cases when it would be easier to look the
other way. As parents, we try to convey to our children the importance of making morally correct decisions and "doing the right
thing" even when taking action is difficult. Yet in specific instances
when our own children are in a position to intervene, it is easy to
succumb to the fear that their safety or reputation may be compro-
mised and to discourage them from taking action.

In truth, however, we can expect our children to act with courage
only if we do so ourselves. When your child comes to you with an
account of an act of cruelty that he has witnessed, he will be looking
to you to demonstrate the appropriate behavior in such a situation.
Giving in to your protective impulse and advising him to stay out of
it or to refuse to be named as a witness will send a strong message
that it's best to look to your own needs when others are in trouble—

not a lesson that most parents want their children to learn. Instead, look at such situations as a valuable learning experience that can provide the following benefits to your child:

Building courage. By talking with your child about how to intervene successfully in a bullying relationship, or how to get adult help if he realizes that he cannot handle the situation on his own, you can support his efforts to develop the necessary courage to stand up for what's right. Certainly, no child should intervene directly in a situation when he feels he may be physically harmed, but how to get help without endangering one's own safety is one of the most important skills a parent can teach a child.

Saving others. Many brutal types of bullying start with minor incidents that often occur in group settings. A casual insult one day may escalate to a cruel beating or a flaming months later. By stepping in early with a disarming comment or action, your child can have the satisfaction of preventing greater harm to the victim, other children and even the bully himself.

Strengthening self-esteem. We all feel great about ourselves when we've done a good deed. When your child acts to stop bullying behavior, he knows he's accomplished something difficult and outstanding. He can also see the real improvements he has created in the life of the victim and, to some degree, in his social environment. Chances are that the victim and most onlookers will hold him in higher regard in the future. Not only may he win a few new friends through his actions, but his opinion of himself will no doubt improve.

Letting pride, not guilt, in. Children who do not step in to stop bullying frequently suffer afterwards from guilt, faltering friendships and lowered self-esteem. If the victim's suffering is particularly acute or the episode especially violent, your child may recall it for the rest of his life with a great deal of discomfort and regret. If he chooses and is helped to take action, on the other hand, he will not only enjoy a feeling of personal pride for having worked to remedy the situation, but he will set the stage for an increase in positive interactions in the future. A 1995 study by Wendy Silverman and colleagues at Case Western Reserve University showed that the most frequent and intense worry of children in grades two through six is that they will be personally harmed or attacked by others. Students' refusal to tolerate bullying helps decrease this concern, allowing for a more positive attitude toward school, improved social relationships and better behavior overall.

TALKING WITH YOUR CHILD
ABOUT BULLYING

"So, Sharon, are you going to Sarah's party on Saturday?"

"No, Mom . . . I don't know. I guess, maybe."

"What's the problem?"

"Nothing. Well . . . okay, there is a problem. Sarah invited me but she didn't invite Theresa. Every other girl in our class got invited. Sarah hates Theresa because she got to be captain of the baseball team. And, you know, Theresa's a friend of mine."

"So you think you shouldn't go to the party either?"

"I don't know, Mom. I can't decide. But Sarah's been pretty mean to her. She keeps saying nasty things about her family and she tries to make sure no one else is friends with her."

Conversations like this spring up now and then in most families, as nearly every child witnesses bullying of some kind sooner or later. In many cases, it can be quite difficult for a child to know whether or how to intervene, since the same issues that concern you about physical safety or social risk are most likely on her mind as well. You can help your child a great deal in managing such situations by talking her through her options and helping her understand more about why bullying happens, how it works and why and how it should be stopped.

Why Are They So Mean?

Your child can't deal effectively with bullying behavior until she learns to recognize it and to understand some of the underlying dynamics involved. Brief, positive, age-appropriate guidance regarding such issues as sharing, listening and using words rather than physical actions to express feelings can and should begin as early as toddlerhood—even before your child is able to fully understand them. (Your younger toddler may not know exactly what you mean when you say that what she did hurt Molly's feelings, but she will respond to your unhappy expression and tone of voice.) As she begins to observe and take note of other children's experiments with physical aggression, name-calling and social manipulation in preschool or kindergarten, discuss such incidents with her—focusing not on whose fault the incident was but on what each child (and your child) might have done to correct it.

If you have talked with your young child in this way, she will probably have a pretty good idea of what is appropriate and what isn't (at least in others, if not always in herself) by age four or five. She may even have labeled certain children as mean or thoughtless, announcing when she comes home from school that one child "always hits" or another "never wants to play with me." At this early age, your child will not be able to understand much about the dynamics of such behavior beyond "Dave must feel mad. He needs to practice using his words to tell people how he feels," or "Maybe Stacy thinks it's funny to say 'No!' when someone wants to play. But it makes the other person feel bad, doesn't it? It's better when everyone is having fun." Rather than attempt to go into much depth explaining such behavior (which is often spontaneous and unpremeditated in any case), focus on teaching your child some reliable responses to unkind actions when she sees them. Explain to her—many times and in many different contexts—that if she sees a child getting hurt, she should "always tell a grownup." If she is frustrated by a playmate's unfair behavior, remind her that "it takes time to learn all the rules" and show her how to suggest a compromise (by suggesting a pillow fight instead of a fistfight), negotiate (agreeing to play what he wants first if he will play what the others want afterwards) and distract (start a new activity, thus effectively ending the conflict). Read children's books about bullying and briefly talk with her about the issues involved afterwards.

Meanwhile, if you notice that one child in the class seems isolated and picked on, suggest some ways that your child might want to play with him. If your child doesn't particularly like this potential victim herself, help her find an interest they have in common. (Perhaps they will find that they both like to play dress-up or to invent new "recipes" in the kitchen.) With your child's permission, invite the other child over for a play date. Your efforts to include an isolated member of the class may not only help that child avoid social victimization but will give your child valuable lessons in how to extend kindness to others and improve her own social environment.

Building on Early Knowledge

As your child enters elementary school and begins to observe bigger kids picking on smaller ones, groups ganging up on individuals, and bullies singling out children who happen to be shy or otherwise vulnerable, you can begin discussing the dynamics of bullying more fully with her. Point out the fact that bullies always select a victim who is in some way weaker than they are. Ask her how the victim responded, and use this as a way to talk about how a victim's response can encourage or discourage more harassment. Discuss what effect the presence of adults has on bullies' behavior, and point out how damaging it is when teachers, parents or other authority figures—as well as other children—choose to look the other way. Later in this chapter I will discuss specific ways in which your child can begin to intervene when such abuse is going on—but it is also important for her to begin thinking about how bullying works so that she can begin to understand why it should be stopped and how it might be.

By the time your child enters middle school, she is likely to find herself surrounded by instances of social manipulation ("Nobody sit with Maureen in the lunchroom!"), emotional cruelty ("Where do you get those clothes?") and physical or even sexual harassment. She may decide to discuss some of these events with you, particularly if you are able to listen and comment in a calm, objective manner. This is a good time to bring up the subject of the pressure to conform and its damaging effects on many children this age. If she claims to admire a dominant—and dominating—group of kids in her class, ask her what exactly she likes about them and whether she believes they would stick up for her if she were ever in serious trouble or in a socially embarrassing situation. If she mentions an incident in which one child was ganged up on by several others, talk also about how hard it is to be singled out and ridiculed, and ask your child how she thinks the situation might have been remedied. Your child may complain that her teachers never do anything about bullying. If so, ask her how you and she might change that situation, or how she might deliberately call such harassment to the attention of school personnel in the future.

Don't forget the power of your own reminiscences and comments on recent events. Over dinner, talk about a bullying incident you yourself experienced, a movie you've seen or an article you've read relating to bullying, and encourage your children to debate the relevant issues, such as "What if you don't like the victim, either? Do you still have to help him out?" "What if you like the person who's bullying and want him to like you?" and "What if the victim will never know she's been gossiped about? Do you still have to do something to stop it?" Demonstrating your interest and involvement in these ways will not only help your child think through what is right and wrong in terms of social interaction, but may encourage her to ask for your input when dealing with incidents as they occur.

By the middle of high school, your child will probably have grown less enchanted with the unkind cliques in her class and less patient with individuals who haven't learned to acceptably channel their aggression. She may still witness or even experience many instances of bullying, but at this age she is less likely to describe most instances to you and ideally will be better equipped to deal with them herself. At this age, she may become more aware of life's "big issues," and her larger world may start to expand. She may become more interested in philosophical or moral ideas relating to violence against others and develop positive, idealistic attitudes about how people should interact. Encourage her to explore these ideas in as many different ways as possible—choosing "political bullying" as a subject for a term paper, perhaps, or bringing up the topic of bullying and other forms of violence for discussion in her religious youth group or among her friends. This is also a wonderful time to urge your child to take real action against bullying whenever and wherever it occurs in her environment. Talk with her whenever you can about how much it would mean—for her as well as any victims—to refuse to tolerate flaming on the Internet, practical jokes at school or violence in the neighborhood.

When Your Child Is a Witness

You can talk with your child almost any time about bullying in a general, moral or even philosophical sense. When she has witnessed a specific incident, however, and is concerned about whether or not to intervene, you will need to walk her through the scenario to decide what her best options are. Given that the two of you have agreed that witnessing a bullying incident and doing nothing is rarely (if ever) acceptable, she will need to know what to say or whom to contact to help the victim and discourage bullying while protecting herself.

First, you will need to help your child assess the social and physical risks of stepping in. If the incident was minor and was not just the latest in a long string of incidents, your child's well-placed objection next time may discourage the bully and the other onlookers with little risk to anyone. If the attacks have escalated, the bully will feel more powerful in this context (and more likely to turn on anyone who intervenes), and other group members may be more likely to support him. Ask your child to describe the history behind the event she witnessed, the circumstances in which it occurred and her own opinion about the risk involved in intervening. If she tells you that she is afraid of being hurt, ask why. (She may have witnessed others being hurt by the same person—a legitimate reason for concern—or may simply be generally fearful of such situations, something the two of you can discuss.) Talk with her about what she feels she needs to do to be safe in this situation.

Your child needs to analyze the dynamics of the situation as well, including the question of where she fits in in relation to the victim and the bully. Since bullies rarely attack others whom they perceive as socially equal to or stronger than themselves, your child will need to consider her social status compared to the aggressor. Again, if your child is at least as popular, she may be able to discourage the bully with a humorous or distracting comment or action. ("Come on, Joe, pick on someone your own age. Let's go play video games.") If she is physically smaller or socially weaker than the bully, intervening is riskier. Ask your child to describe the bully to you—his size and strength, his level of popularity, his history of bullying and whether he has been in trouble at school before for aggressive acts. You may also want to talk about the other witnesses to the incident. Will these onlookers back up your child if she needs help?

Finally, you and your child need to discuss the reliability of the adult support where the bullying is taking place. A school with an anti-bullying campaign already in place is obviously among the easiest places for a bystander to intervene successfully. A school where, according to your child, "the teachers never listen even though we tell them about Joe all the time" is a higher-risk place to intervene, since your child may find herself without protection after she has made her move.

Children being children, it is not always the case that your child's assessments of risk will be accurate and reliable. Many children believe they are stronger and more socially powerful than they actually are. Many feel that teachers are unsympathetic when they simply have never been asked to intercede. Difficult as it can be at times, you will need to use your judgment in helping your child decide the best course of action to take.

How Safe Is It?

Ideally, your child will have witnessed an early attack on a particular victim, in which case it may be a simple matter to prevent further attacks from occurring—or her own social status will be high enough for her to intervene without fear of reprisal. If she is willing to intervene but still feels a little uneasy, offer to back her up by talking with teachers or other parents ahead of time or standing by the phone around the time she expects the confrontation to take place. It may help for the two of you to look at the intervention as a kind of social experiment. Your child can decide to try a certain comment or response ("I hate mash notes. They're stupid. How would you like it if I wrote one about you?") and see how it works. Afterwards, the two of you can discuss the results and perhaps fashion a better response for next time.

In some cases, the two of you may agree that the risk of intervening is simply too high. (Certainly this is *always* the case if you or your child believe that she may be at risk of physical harm.) If so, be sure to respect your child's judgment (after all, she was there) and refrain from criticizing her for hesitating to confront a bully when another child is being hurt. Instead, let her know how proud you are that she has decided to do anything at all, and discuss some alternative actions with her. You may suggest that she leave the room if the incident occurs again, for example. (She can then contact an adult to handle the situation instead, as described below.) You may advise her to talk with the victim about ideas for helping to correct the situation next time. You may be tempted to step in and intervene directly yourself—by talking to your child's teacher or even calling the bully's parents—but it's generally best to let your child try to resolve the issue on her own, even if she needs to rely on teachers, camp counselors or other adults to do so. Not only will such an experience add to her confidence next time such an event occurs, but she will be able to savor for herself the wonderful sense of having acted positively to help another person— positive reinforcement that she deserves.

Of course taking action on the spot isn't a good idea in every situation. Your child needs to know when it's safe to intervene and when it isn't. Before an incident occurs, be sure your child understands that she should:

- Not interfere directly if she is alone and her own status is less than the bully's
- Look for other witnesses to back her up
- Never attempt to physically combat a bully
- Know when to call on an adult for help

Knowing that abuse is taking place and allowing it to continue is morally compromising to anyone—even to a very young child. If your child has decided that intervening directly in a bullying relationship is simply too risky—or if she was faced with a situation in which she could have intervened but didn't—she is likely to feel bad. If this is the case with your child, be sure to talk with her about her feelings of guilt or fear. Let her know that many people, even adults, feel bad about avoiding conflict or not helping out. Remind her gently that the past cannot be undone, and that part of life is learning to do better. Then help her to look forward by reviewing the situation with her and generating some ideas of what to do next time. There are a number of ways to stop bullying, wherever it is found, other than directly confronting the aggressor. Be sure that your child has a few such techniques in mind next time she finds herself in such a situation.

"BUT WHAT CAN I *DO*?" HOW YOUR CHILD CAN STOP BULLYING WITHOUT BEING BULLIED

Standing by and allowing bullying to take place is not an option for children who are concerned for everyone's health and safety, including their own. If your child has decided that he is willing and able to intervene in a bullying situation, or wants to consider what he might do next time, discuss with him the following options:

Name the Crime

Sometimes just pointing out what's happening can be enough to stop a bullying action before it gains momentum. Your kindergartner or young child can be taught to say, "We're not supposed to hit," or "That's a bad word," if he is attacked or harassed, and to leave the scene if the bullying continues. An elementary school child can confront older bullies with "Why are you picking on a little kid?" or "You're not supposed to play with us first-graders." Middle-schoolers may be able to deal with gossip or social manipulation simply by saying, "That's not true," or "It's mean to leave one person out." All teenagers should feel comfortable saying, "She doesn't have to go anywhere with you," and "Just because he's different doesn't mean you can pick on him."

Suggest an Alternative

Sometimes bullying situations develop because no one involved knows how to stop them. As early as possible, start showing your child ways to provide distractions or alternative activities that can prevent violence from escalating. Since young children are easily distractible, your child may be able to stop aggressive behavior by coming up with a silly joke or a hug, or suggesting a new game to play. Older children may be able to introduce a new idea into conversation—interrupting speculation about an absent person's sex life, for example, with a remark about what he heard on the news about adolescent sexual behavior or something he read about the sex life of chimpanzees. A child who senses that a violent situation is building up on the playground may suggest a game of baseball. A simple "Hey, let's go over to my house" may work to stymie bullying tendencies after school.

Tell an Adult

No one wants to be a tattletale. If your child has the social strength and skills to stop bullying on his own when he sees it, so much the better. However, there are many instances when bullies outnumber or otherwise overwhelm victims and witnesses alike. In these cases, your child needs to feel comfortable calling on adults for help, and he needs to have some specific adults in mind.

Before such an incident occurs, talk with your child about whom he might ask for help in his classroom, on the playground, on the school bus and in the neighborhood. Make sure he has a reliable list of adults in mind. Allow him to choose the adults he feels most comfortable with, even if you don't agree with all his choices. It's more important for him to feel comfortable approaching an adult if he finds himself in danger than it is for him to observe such traditional channels as telling his teacher (rather than a counselor) or coming to you (rather than his uncle).

Help the Victim

Whether or not your child is able to intervene successfully in a bullying attempt as it is taking place, he may be able to help the victim in private later on. Since bullies tend to prey on those who are socially isolated, your child may be able to do an enormous amount of good simply by talking with the victim, spending time with her and bolstering her self-confidence in any way he can. If the victim is afraid to walk home from school alone, your child may volunteer to accompany her. If she lacks a fulfilling social life, he may be able to get her involved in some of the activities he enjoys. By getting to know the victim a little better, he may also be able to recognize danger signs that will alert him to seek help from adults. Many a potential suicide victim has been saved by a concerned friend's intervention. As your child approaches adolescence, try hard to keep the lines of communication open so you can help him spot signs of chronic abuse or victimization in others. Talk with him specifically about what signs to look for in terms of depression, drug abuse, sexual abuse and so on, and talk about ways in which he might help a victimized friend who refuses to get help for herself.

Help the Bully

It is painful to see one's friends engage in cruel behavior, especially when your child begins to feel it's necessary to choose between the behavior and the friends. He may be able to avoid this choice by talking his friends out of their bullying ways. A simple "Let him alone, he's not hurting anyone" sometimes works if your child has sufficient social status in the group. A joke or diversion can also stem any violence before it gets worse. Afterwards, your child may consider warning his friends about how much trouble they'll get in if they continue their harassment. If he comes across any information about an outright attack (whether physical or social) he will have to consider how to report this information to a responsible adult and to the potential victim.

Enlist an Influential Buddy

As I have pointed out, social and physical strength can be important when confronting a bully. If your child feels powerless facing the prevalence of bullying in his environment or the continuous bullying of one particular child, he may benefit from another's strength. By approaching one of the bully's physical or social equals—someone who is respected or tolerated by the bully but does not share her abusive tendencies—and asking her to help protect the victim, your child may be able to use combined strength to

---

"GOODY-GOODY!"

Many children hesitate to stop a friend who is bullying because they fear they will be called a goody-goody or similarly insulted. If your child fears this response, suggest the following responses for him to consider:

- "So? What's wrong with that?"
- "I would stand up for you, too, if it was you."
- "I don't want you to get in trouble."
- "Look, I'm trying to have a good time and it's not fun to watch other kids get hurt. I'm out of here."

stop the cruelty. Numbers can be powerful, too—particularly among adolescents—and your child may be able to appeal to other onlookers for support. With enough peer pressure to stop victimizing others, a bully may decide that her activities are not rewarding enough and give them up. Meanwhile, your child may even find that the act of rescuing a victim as a group not only solves the immediate problem but makes new friendships possible, and improves the social climate in some small way as well.

"TAKE THAT!"
BULLY INTERVENTION IN THE MEDIA

Bullying incidents appear frequently in movies and television shows designed for children, and it is almost inevitable that your child will witness victims' and onlookers' responses to aggression onscreen as well as in real life. In most cases, the victim and his supporters triumph over the bad guys by giving back to the bullies what they gave—only ten times worse. As the bullies receive their comeuppance, the music typically rises to a triumphant crescendo and the camera cuts ecstatically between the surprised, outraged face of the bully and the delighted smiles and high-five exchanges of the avengers.

Such "eye for an eye" scenarios, in which a victim and well-meaning onlookers carry out elaborate schemes for revenge, are all about wish fulfillment and are deeply satisfying to their young viewers. Yet, if not addressed, they can skew a child's perception of the risk involved in intervening herself in real-life bullying situations. If you allow your child to enjoy such entertainment (and it is hard to avoid), be sure to counter its negative messages with comments about how different things are in real life. Ask, for example, what would happen at your child's school if someone responded

(continued)

to a bullying incident by locking the bully in the boiler room. Explain to your child how violence is created for the movies—with scripts, actors and stunt men and women—and make sure he understands that real bullies in real life hurt kids with real fists. Remark on how amazing it was that none of the adults in the movie seemed to notice the bullying that was taking place and that none of the kids asked the adults for help—since teaming up with adults would have considerably lowered their risk. Ask your child which adults he could rely on in a similar situation and how they might respond in more effective ways.

In the end, there is nothing wrong and much that is healthy about working out anxieties about violence through stories and film. Just make sure your child truly understands the difference between fantasy and fact when it comes to dealing with bullying in his own life—and that in real life the good guys sometimes lose.

FIGHTING BULLYING AT SCHOOL, IN THE NEIGHBORHOOD AND IN THE WORLD

"We are a group of sixth-graders and our organization is all about positive peer pressure," a student writes. "We want to start a pen-pal program to help kids help each other." Perhaps it is not so surprising, considering how upsetting most children find bullying in their schools and neighborhoods, but I have been deeply impressed over the years at how active and creative some children can become in combating cruelty among their peers. If you have made a point throughout your child's life to identify bullying situations where you find them and to help your child find acceptable ways to stop harassment, you may be gratified to see her interest in this area expand as she enters her teens. In Chapter 9, I will describe some of the school anti-bullying programs that have been founded by students in recent years—and that have proved surprisingly effective in changing these schools' social climate. If your own child is upset about the level of cruelty currently tolerated at her school or in her neighborhood, talk with her about starting her own anti-violence club or campaign. Such activities can put her in touch with like-minded teenagers and even adults who may continue to provide valuable friendship and support for years to come. They can also show her how ethical convictions can be put to practical use in the world at large—through community activism, effective communication and even government intervention. Even if your child decides to focus on changing the status quo in less formal ways, working with her can only help you in your efforts to guide her toward a more thoughtful and ethically active adulthood.

CHAPTER SEVEN

EMPOWERING
YOUR CHILD

IT IS A PAINFUL EXPERIENCE for any parent when a child comes home with a bloody nose, torn clothes or other evidence that he has been bullied by his peers. If you discover that your child has been harmed or harassed, your first impulse may be to rush out and hurt or punish his attacker. Yet, from your child's point of view, taking that kind of control over the situation may be the very worst thing you could do. Your child's protests—"Mom, I can handle this!" or "Please, Dad, don't get involved!"—signal more than a desire not to be embarrassed or babied. A targeted attack or harassment from a peer represents a gross violation of a child's developing sense of self. He will recover more fully if you help him respond successfully on his own.

The key word here, of course, is *successfully*. Your victimized child will need your listening ear, careful guidance and follow-up support if he is to triumph in a bullying situation. Since bullies nearly always choose victims who are weaker in some way, real change will be required before the harassment can be stopped. This is not to say that your child is at fault, or that *he* is the one who must change. It will be necessary, however, for you to review the dynamics of the situation with him and decide on a different approach. In this chapter, I will take you step by step through the process of assessing the situation, helping your child determine whether he is capable of handling it himself, choosing and rehearsing a good response and monitoring the results. I will also suggest effective ways you can step in if this proves necessary, and to see that your child finds better ways to manage social interaction in his day-to-day life.

"WHAT HAPPENED?"

In order to help your child find a way to manage a bullying situation on her own, you will first need to gather all the information you can about the incident or series of incidents that have taken place: what happened, the context in which the bullying occurred, how your child responded and how any adults or other onlookers acted as well. It is not always easy to get this kind of information from a child who has been involved in such a conflict. As I pointed out in Chapter 4, your child may feel ashamed of being singled out for harassment, guilty because she suspects she invited the attack in some way, or fearful of a strong emotional reaction or negative judgment from you. You will need to convey your willingness to listen to what she has to say, calmly and with an open mind. It may help to tell her about a time when you were victimized, so that she will know you really do understand how she feels. Make clear to her that you are not trying to make a case against the bully so that you can go after him or otherwise interfere. You are just collecting the information you need to help her decide on the best course of action *she* can take—action that may include asking for help or support in a way that feels good for her. If you learn that other children or adults witnessed the event, and you feel you do not yet have all the relevant facts, consider talking with these witnesses about what they observed and soliciting their opinions about the situation. It is best to do this only if you have your child's consent. If she senses that you are going behind her back, she may withhold the trust you need to help her solve this situation. Explain to her your reasons for wanting others' input. Tell her that you are trying to gain as clear an understanding as possible about the bully's motivation and personality so you can help her decide on the best response. If she continues to resist, ask yourself (and perhaps her) why. Is she worried that others will reveal things she hasn't shared with you? (If so, it's best that she divulge this information herself.) Is she concerned that others will tease or criticize her for allowing a parent to step in? (If this is the case, you can assure her that your conversations will be private and that you will limit them to adults only or to the people she approves.) Any way that you can offer her a sense of control will help.

If, in the end, your child simply sees such discussions as a further violation of her privacy, you may have to back off and satisfy yourself with the information already at hand. Again, applying too much pressure can cause a backlash effect that will defeat the purpose of further inquiry. In the meantime, even if you are unable to put together the entire picture, you can reassure yourself that your child is aware of it and can adapt your guidelines accordingly.

Once you have as full an account as possible of what actually occurred, you and your child can put the facts of the situation to the "bully" test. Ask yourselves the following questions about what happened:

- Was the act intentional, or perceived as intentional?
  (*You might ask your child, "Did she mean to hurt your feelings?"*)
- Was it of a degrading or offensive nature?
  (*"Were you offended by what he did?"*)
- Did it occur without apparent or sufficient provocation?
  (*"What do you think made her want to hurt you?"*)

- Did your child object clearly to this treatment? If so, was the act repeated or continued?
  (*"Did you tell her to stop? Did she?"*)
- Was there a real or perceived imbalance in power or strength between the attacker and your child?
  (*"Was she older, stronger, more popular, or with a bunch of other bullies?"*)

As you and your child search for answers to these questions, you may find that the incident she describes is not clearly a bullying situation. Your child may have been subject to teasing, for example, but the teasing may have been meant in fun and your child may have overreacted to some degree. Or a teenager may have made an awkward sexual pass at your daughter but perhaps did not intend to harass her. Your child may come to realize in the telling that she is only now attaching names to her feelings (resentment, shame)—though at the time she may have laughed halfheartedly, pretending to go along with it instead of asking the aggressor to stop. Defining the event for what it is may help her understand what went wrong and how best to avoid such conflicts in the future. In the meantime, whatever the situation—bullying or not—she needs help responding appropriately and is relying on you for nonjudgmental guidance and support.

"CAN YOU HANDLE THIS?"

Once you and your child have carefully discussed what happened and why, you can begin to assess your child's ability to respond on his own. The idea is to employ his strengths and work around his weaknesses. Again, it is important to communicate to your child that you are not judging his *inherent* strength but his readiness to attack this particular problem at this particular point in his life. His age, size, personality, interests, stage of development and level of experience all contribute to this readiness. His basic character is not the issue.

First, it is necessary to consider what *the bully perceives* as your child's weakness—the point of vulnerability that she has tried to exploit—and discuss with your child whether there are any immediate ways to address that issue and make himself less vulnerable. Was your child walking home alone when he was attacked? If so, would his problem be solved if some friends, a sibling or an adult joined him on the walk? Is your child shy and thus vulnerable to taunts and other types of harassment? If so, perhaps he could write an honest letter to the most approachable of the bullies, or ask a more assertive friend to help defend him. Is he smaller or younger than the bully? Then he may simply be able to get help from an adult or a larger or older friend or sibling. Does he respond to bullying by crying, acting fearful or otherwise unintentionally rewarding his abusers? Perhaps some empathetic discussion of this behavior and rehearsal (see below) will help him deal with bullying in more effective ways.

It is important that your child not feel that in addressing the bullying, he forgoes his rights as an individual or his sense of self. For example, a teenaged boy who has become the target of vicious gossip because he happens to like a particular girl should not respond by avoiding the girl. Rather, he might decide to confront the bully with witnesses present and ask for an explanation, or he may prefer to ask his friends to refute the rumors on his behalf. Such solutions can solve the problem without impinging on your child's freedom. The final question anyone should ask himself before he decides on an action should be "Is this response fair to me? Will I feel better about myself if I act in this way?"

You and your child should consider also what other strengths your child possesses or has access to that protect him against bully-

---

**HOW TO CHANGE A BULLY'S BEHAVIOR**

Every bullying situation is different, and you and your child will need to consider all aspects of the situation before deciding how to solve his particular problem. Following are some basic suggestions on which to base your child's plan of action:

WHAT TO DO	WHAT _NOT_ TO DO
▪ Ask the bully to stop.	▪ Fight back physically.
▪ Get your friends to help.	▪ Have someone else hit the bully.
▪ Let adults know what is happening	▪ Respond by crying or acting upset.
▪ Remind adults if you are still being bullied.	▪ Stop going to school.

---

ing. If he is experiencing racial, religious or sexual harassment, he may be able to connect with school clubs or organizations specifically designed to offer him help and support. If he is physically small (and thus picked on) but witty (and thus probably at least somewhat popular), he may be able to use humor to deflect the bully's attack. If he works on the school newspaper, he may decide to write an article about his experience, not necessarily naming names but garnering support for his cause. If he is a creative or artistic type, he may be able to express his feelings about the bullying through his art, thus lowering his level of fear or anxiety to such a degree that the bully no longer considers him a satisfying target. Or he may have other interests or involvements that, if stepped up, can distract him from the incident and make him unavailable for bullying.

It is possible that you and your child cannot readily identify the trait or behavior that has attracted this bully. If so, make an effort to observe your child in social situations such as Scout meetings or parties to see if you can figure out where his vulnerability lies. If you

---

"HIT HER BACK!"
WHAT'S WRONG WITH REVENGE

Countless movies, TV shows and our personal stories attest that the best way to respond to a bully is to fight back and win. Yet experience tells us that what more often happens is that the victim is victimized even worse than before—just as she had feared. Furthermore, fighting back endorses the use of violence among children and may even violate the instincts of a child who knows better than to use physical violence against her foes.

If your first instinct, when confronted with evidence that your child has been physically bullied, is to sign her up for karate or some other type of self-defense course, ask yourself what your purpose is in doing so. While such classes may be a good idea for a child who can use a confidence boost, they should not be suggested for the purpose of eventually beating up the bully. On the contrary, it is your responsibility as a parent to hold up the bully's use of physical aggression as a negative example—and to strongly endorse the defense-only, last-resort philosophy of most self-defense disciplines. Your child's goal for solving the bullying problem should be justice, not revenge.

---

believe you may have found the key to the puzzle, share your suspicions with your child as tactfully as possible and offer to help him work out ways to solve the problem. Don't forget to point out that he played a part in generating the solution by talking about it with you. An important part of self-empowerment for children consists of knowing when and why to talk things over with an adult.

"HOW WILL YOU RESPOND?"

Once you and your child have discussed the bullying incident and assessed your child's strengths and vulnerabilities, it is time to decide together how she will respond. The bottom line for all such conversations must be that if your child is in physical danger, she *cannot* be allowed to handle the situation alone and adults *must* intervene. You can discuss with your child what you or another adult plans to do in this case (a number of approaches will be discussed in Chapters 8 and 9), but in no event should a child be allowed to knowingly expose herself to physical abuse. Keep in mind the fact that bullies nearly always choose a weaker victim. The fact that they have chosen your child means they are confident they can beat her.

If the harassment is not physical, you and your child can discuss what method to try first in dealing with the bully. Your child may choose to avoid him, to make sure she herself is part of a group and never isolated, to respond in assertive ways (see box on page 123), to use humor to disarm the bully in others' presence, or to use one of the other avenues for self-defense described in the previous section. To come up with ideas that are appropriate for your child's situation, consider the following types of response:

• **Verbal.** An assertive statement, retort or joke that will sway witnesses' opinion in favor of your child.

• **Social.** The support of friends; avoidance of the bully; involvement in other activities that remove your child from the bully's sphere of influence.

• **Creative or intellectual.** Writing a newspaper article; creating a short story, play or work of art that expresses how it feels to be bullied and renders your child less emotionally vulnerable.

- **Behavioral.** Working consciously on social skills and concepts (personal space, turn-taking, etc.) to avoid provoking a bullying response.

- **Professional.** Calling on an authority figure such as a teacher, counselor or school resource officer for help and support.

The choice your child makes should reflect her strengths and resources as well as her feelings about what would be effective and morally correct. Your child should also understand that whatever approach she chooses is a first option and nothing more. She should feel free to change her mind and respond in another way at any time if she feels the need. If she decides she wants or needs adult help, she should feel free to ask for it and know how to do so. It's a good idea to discuss a Plan B ahead of time. Your child will be more confident knowing that if Plan A doesn't work, it isn't the end of the world. You'll keep trying until the problem is solved.

GETTING READY

Once you and your child have chosen what you feel is the best response, it is time to start practicing for the actual face-to-face encounter. The more he prepares in this way, the more confident he will feel as he carries out his response and the less vulnerable he will be to further harassment. Work with your child to come up with actual scenarios that may occur. Agree on what the bully might say or do, listen to your child's description of how he might respond and give your opinion on what the bully might do or say as a result. This type of preparation works best if you and your child actually rehearse these scenarios, alternating the roles of bully and victim until you have played out all likely interchanges and your child feels comfortable with what he plans to say and do. If anxieties surface—on your child's part or your own—it's important to work through them now and find acceptable solutions. If your child is amenable (more likely with a younger child than with a teenager), ask other family members to witness your rehearsals and offer critiques. Siblings or other relatives may be able to offer last-minute advice based on familiarity with the bully or his milieu or their own childhood experiences.

Working together as a family in this way to create the best response to bullying can help transform such an experience from a painful, private exercise into a difficult but interesting social experiment. By working as a team, you and your child can diminish the emotional impact of the bullying incident while strengthening your own bond. Such strong, unflinching support from his family may be your child's greatest weapon in regaining and maintaining his self-esteem.

THE POWER OF POSITIVE ASSERTIONS

Sometimes, all it takes to stop a bully is a clear statement—preferably in front of supportive witnesses—that her behavior is not welcome or appreciated. Aggressive responses (returning an insult, threatening the bully, etc.) may lead to an escalation of violence, but rational questions or comments that address the conflict itself may stop the bully in her tracks. Your child may benefit from practicing the following assertive statements before his next encounter with a bully:

- "Why would you say that?"
- "What makes you think I'm that way?"
- "Who told you that?"
- "I'm sorry you feel that way, but it's not true."
- "If we don't agree on something, can we just talk about it reasonably?"

"DID IT WORK?"

Talking about a response to bullying is one thing, but it's another to send your child off to school knowing she is going to confront a bully that day. It may help to remind yourself (and, possibly, your child) that she is well prepared and has a variety of options from which to choose, depending on the circumstances she encounters. Assure her that she is doing the right thing and that you will be available by phone (or perhaps physically nearby) if she needs you. Be sure she knows the names of adults she can call on for help, and make sure she understands exactly how and where to find them. You should have on hand the phone numbers of the bully's parents and any appropriate adults such as her teacher, school counselor, coach or bus driver. In many cases (as we will see in later chapters) it makes sense for these adults to at least be made aware of what is going on ahead of time, even if you are not asking them to do anything at this point. If the adults in charge know that an encounter between two children may take place, they can keep an eye out for trouble and stop any serious abuse before it gets out of hand.

Once your child has interacted with the bully and has reported the results, discuss with her how effective her response turned out to be. If it stopped the bullying, this is certainly cause for celebration. Congratulate her on having competently handled the situation on her own and be sure she experiences the satisfaction of a job well done. If the bully continued his harassment, remind your child that she did her best and that she still has other options she can try. Keep in mind the fact that she is likely to feel doubly disappointed that she failed to control the situation in this instance, and be sure to point out that this is a difficult challenge that even adults have a hard time overcoming.

Next, you and your child will need to reconsider whether she would still like to proceed with the agreed-on Plan B, to revise this plan according to what she learned during this most recent encounter, or allow you or another adult to intervene. Even if your child cannot be the final arbiter in this matter (that is your job as her parent), she must absolutely be a part of the decision. Not only can she provide the most detailed information about what works and what doesn't, she also needs this opportunity to reestablish her sense of control over her life and her environment.

WHEN TO STEP IN

Sometimes children need help solving problems. If your child has exhausted all the options he cares to exercise and the bully is still harassing him, it is time for you to step in. Still, you should discuss with your child what you plan to do and whom you will approach about this problem. You may decide (ideally, with your child's approval) to confront the bully, his parents or another adult such as a teacher or policeman. Later chapters will help you manage such actions successfully. For now, it's important for your child to understand that you are not "taking over" and that your participation does not mean that he has "failed." Tell him tactfully, "I think you have done all you can do about this. You've done a great job, but you need a little adult support." or "Let me see if I can help a little. I'll try to make sure almost no one knows." Remind him that his family support system is one of his many strengths, and it's time for him to put it to use in handling this situation.

If the bullying continues and your child seems strongly invested in continuing the battle without adult intervention, you may want to consider the possibility that on some (probably unconscious) level your child doesn't *want* the bullying to end. Negative attention can be less painful for some children than no attention at all. Your child may provoke the bully just to be noticed—but then receive more attention than he would like. If you believe this is the case, intervening directly may not help much in the long run, since your child is likely to choose another bully to provoke if this one is stopped. Instead, try talking with your child about what kind of attention he would like to get from others. Make it clear that asking for any attention from a bully may be asking for trouble. Help him figure out ways to get his classmates to focus positively on him—by doing favors for others, participating in clubs or other activities or even helping another child assert her rights when she's being bullied. Communicate your willingness to intervene whenever necessary, but make it clear to your child that he must do his part in maintaining social relationships, too.

AN EMPOWERED CHILD

While a bullying situation requires immediate, focused attention on a child's social strengths and bolstering of her abilities, it is important to look for a variety of ways to empower your child at other times, too. In some cases, you may hear about your child's experiences with bullying long after the fact, or never learn about them at all. By helping her improve her social skills and general self-confidence, you can prevent some of these difficulties from ever taking place and help her deal with the others more successfully.

One way to protect your child from bullying is to educate her about the strengths she already has. If you are concerned that she may be singled out because of her race, religious background, sexual orientation or gender, for example, teach her about her civil rights and to take pride in her heritage. Encourage her to join organizations for children or teenagers that support her rights and interests. If she is an avid chess player or is good at track, compare her positively to others her age and offer to help her enter competitions. Even if she is very shy, from a modest background or otherwise disadvantaged in the status wars among her peers, you can let her know that many accomplished people in the world experienced childhoods similar to her own.

Like most parents, you may see the need for additional training for your child, and there is no harm in offering this support if she is willing to participate. Children who lack self-confidence or are physically small or weak often benefit a great deal from martial arts courses or sports activities. If you feel that your child's communication skills are weak, pay more attention to this at home or talk with her teacher or school counselor about finding a competent speech therapist or other professional who can help her. A girl who is teased for "looking dumpy" or having "bad hair" may appreciate your offer of a professional makeover. However, it is vital to put your child's feelings first. A makeover or some new karate moves will not protect your child from further bullying—only elevating her self-esteem can do that. If your child feels she is being criticized rather than supported, your efforts to empower won't work.

In fact, your loving presence and involvement in your child's life is, in most cases, more effective than all the self-improvement routines money can buy. Take the time to sit down to meals with your child, hang out with her after work or school, and share activities that you both enjoy. Listen to her stories about her day. Show her that you're interested in her dreams and aspirations as well as her anxieties and fears. Provide a welcoming home where she can bring her friends, and do your best to be as accepting of them as you are of her. Her knowledge that you are there for her—that you know and approve of who she is—will provide her with the confidence she needs.

DAILY REMINDERS

Empowering your child doesn't require enormous effort or dramatic gestures on your part. A child's self-confidence rests mostly on the quiet details of her day-to-day interaction with you. Some small but important ways to boost your child's confidence and self-esteem on a daily basis include:

- Talking with her about her ideas, fantasies and strengths.
- Reminding her frequently—through casual remarks, notes in her lunch box and conversations at bedtime, that she is liked and valued. (Be careful that others don't see or hear these reminders, as they may be embarrassing.)
- Asking for and respecting her opinions and decisions, when appropriate.
- Displaying artwork and good report cards prominently, letting her know that her hard work and creativity are valued.
- Giving her tasks to perform that are appropriate to her age and skill level, and complimenting her on a job well done.
- Easing up on your pressure on her to perform. Your child may feel so stressed by a full schedule of activities that she has no energy left over for social and emotional growth.

IF YOUR CHILD IS THE AGGRESSOR

It may seem counterintuitive to state that the aggressors in abusive relationships need empowering, too, but this is the case with children or adolescents who have difficulty managing their anger or frustration in acceptable ways. If your child has been credibly accused of teasing, hurting or otherwise harassing others, he urgently needs your support as he learns to recognize and respond appropriately to his own emotions, respect others' viewpoints and express himself in ways that don't hurt others. (Remember, he may be this way because others have bullied him.) He may need to be taught how to interact with members of the opposite sex without harassing them, resist friends' pressure to bully others and respond nonviolently to his own victimization. Children are not born with these skills—they must be taught. Your child needs to know that there are consequences for his negative behavior, but he also needs to learn some positive alternatives. The sooner you begin working on his emotional education, the more he will benefit and the faster he will learn.

"How Do I Feel?"

We all think we know how we feel from one moment to the next, but it is surprising how frequently people react to situations without fully understanding the emotions that have motivated their behavior. Your child may act upon but not necessarily realize he is experiencing envy, jealousy, resentment, fear or competitiveness. Before he can learn to stop the inappropriate behaviors that spring from these emotions, he must learn to recognize the feelings themselves. You can help him identify and manage his emotions by talking routinely about feelings you have or that you intuit in others. When something upsets or frightens you, say so—not through your actions, but calmly in words. As you watch television with him, comment occasionally on the emotions the show is causing you to feel, or ask him whether he thinks it's "scary" or "too violent." Articulate other family members' emotions, too—"Your little sister didn't get picked for the soccer team, so she's sad." Most important, as you observe his actions at home, comment neutrally on the emotions he is expressing, as in, "You seem angry," or "Do you feel like I treat your sister better than I do you? I'm guessing that would make you mad."

Such comments won't reveal your child's emotional life to him in one fell swoop, but they will get him thinking about his feelings and the way he expresses them to others. You may be able to encourage these early explorations by giving him a journal or otherwise encouraging creative expression, suggesting he join a youth group where he can share his feelings with others like himself, putting him in touch with an older, mentor-type relative or even offering to schedule some appointments for him with a counselor or therapist if he is willing.

"What Makes Me Mad?"

Once your child learns to identify his feelings, he can begin to associate them with specific situations, or triggers. Again, your calm, supportive, nonjudgmental observations may help him in this area. Of course it's not easy for a child—particularly a teenager—to hear this from Mom or Dad. You might find that openly sharing your own emotional triggers—"Put those bills on the counter, okay? They'll just upset me if I look through them now"—make him more aware and accepting of his own. You can also keep an eye out for examples of emotional triggers as you watch television together. ("She's not going over to his house, is she? They always fight when she does that!") Remark—again, kindly rather than critically—on other family members' areas of vulnerability. ("Let's leave Chip alone this afternoon, okay? He had a fight with his girlfriend and he's feeling bad.") All of these observations will allow your child to start thinking about emotional triggers without feeling defensive about his own.

Once you sense that your child has become aware of the issue of emotional triggers, talk with him occasionally about which situations or interactions tend to make him lose his temper. The two of you may notice that he tends to get angry when he's had less than eight hours of sleep, when he has a pile of homework to do, or when he feels pressured to perform. He may lash out when he feels criticized or judged by others or may taunt his siblings or friends when he feels insecure. If you know of a particular situation in which he has been accused of bullying, you may be able to talk about that incident in terms of what triggered his anger and how he might manage his emotions better next time.

"How Do You Think They Feel?"

It may not be easy for your child to recognize and express his own feelings. It may be even harder for him to identify the feelings of others. Empathy—feeling what another feels—is an important early step in stopping aggression toward others. To encourage your child to consider others' feelings and to act accordingly, make a point of commenting on others' feelings and encouraging your child to think about them. Ask him, "How do you think your sister feels right now?" or "Why does that person act that way? What do you imagine they feel like?" This is a good exercise for children of all ages. It's best, in fact, to start talking about other children's feelings when your own child is young and keep up such conversations as he grows.

"What Should I Do When I Get Angry?"

Your child's increasing awareness of his emotional triggers and others' feelings may start him thinking about how to avoid the kinds of aggressive actions that get him into trouble with adults (and, as he grows older, make him less popular among his peers). You can encourage him to expand on his thinking by making and comparing lists of what each of you does when you get angry. Younger children can dictate their lists to you. Your list might include, "Yell, cry, call my best friend and badmouth the person who made me angry." He might list, "Slam my door, kick something, insult the person who made me mad." Looking at these behaviors on paper may spur you to talk about ways you both might respond more positively when you feel negative emotions building up. You can then encourage your child to make a new list (and, perhaps, join him by making your own) of acceptable alternatives such as these:

- Stop and think.
- Take some deep breaths.
- Make a joke out of it.
- Walk away.
- Do something physical but harmless: work out, go for a run or punch a pillow.
- Talk to a trusted friend.
- Write a story or draw a picture about it.
- Tell my dad or mom.
- Tell a teacher.

Older children may not want to write a list (they may think it's stupid). If so, you can simply talk with them about taking different kinds of action—as you would with an adult. Your respectful approach to this discussion will encourage them to think in more adult ways.

Once your child has come up with several alternatives, the two of you can monitor how well it helps him manage his behavior. If you notice him taking a deep breath and stopping to think when he's mad instead of immediately starting to yell, praise him for this effort and consider providing him with a small but significant reward. (Again, it can also help for you to practice this exercise at the same time. Watching you monitor your own behavior may make him feel less defensive and encourage him to monitor his.) Make sure, also, that your child's improved behavior leads to improved results—positive attention from you, an acceptable solution to the conflict and a satisfying expression of his feelings. Gradually, as he practices these new responses and finds that they make his life more pleasant, his self-defeating behaviors should begin to fade away.

"What Does She Mean by That?"

In many cases, conflicts begin between children (as well as adults) because one participant has misunderstood the other's intentions. This is especially common among children, who have limited experience examining their own (and therefore others') emotions. As you encourage your child to think about and manage his feelings, he may naturally begin to understand that he has misinterpreted others' actions in the past—that they were not necessarily insulting him or threatening his safety, or if they were that they did so as a result of their own emotional conflicts. Your child may also begin to note the personal feelings of insecurity that underlie much group harassment and violence, and grow increasingly aware of the dynamics of bullying—that only "weaker" children are victimized and that such aggression solves nothing.

If you see that your child continues, in your view, to misinterpret others' actions in ways that lead to an aggressive response, you will need to take additional steps to help him read others' motivations better. When you yourself interact with him, explain your feelings clearly. Tell him, for example, "I am angry that you didn't study for your biology test and now you've failed it. That makes me sad because I want you to succeed. But I know I can't *make* you do well in school. Is there some way I can help you?" You may also consider seeking out family or individual therapy for this problem if it is ongoing and upsetting to you. Most therapists are experienced at helping clients with such misperceptions and can provide your child with an objective reality check.

"She Gets on My Nerves!"

There are times, of course, when others strain our patience for whatever reason and we don't particularly care how they feel or what their motivation is. Provocative victims—those whose behavior is annoying to many or whose social skills are limited—most often inspire this response. If your child is experiencing this type of challenge, it's best to focus more on his own behavior and less on the other child. Your child must learn which types of behaviors are allowed (asking to be left alone, asking an adult to intervene) and which are not (hitting, yelling or insulting the other child). It is extremely important to *consistently* enforce these limits in nonabusive ways (by, for example, giving a younger child a time out or curbing an older child's privileges). Inconsistent enforcement can be as ineffective as or even worse than neglecting to enforce limits at all.

You will also need to talk frequently with your child about how important it is for each person in a society to enjoy her individual rights and privileges. We must all participate in turn-taking, listening to others' opinions and allowing for other viewpoints if we expect to be treated fairly ourselves. If your child's view of others seems to be somewhat limited or narrow, make an effort to expose him to people, ideas and creative works from cultures other than your own. Be sure to demonstrate your own respect for your child's and others' viewpoints and opinions, no matter how strange or outlandish you consider them. This effort on your part is the best lesson in tolerance you can offer your child.

Is It Teasing or Taunting?

Even when your child has begun to give more thought to others' feelings, motivations and points of view, he may need some help learning the actual words or actions that lead to positive relationships. Sometimes, accusations that he is bullying may be based largely on miscommunication. He may think he's "just kidding around," not realizing how deeply he is hurting another's feelings. He may not know how to express his attraction to another child or adolescent and so he inadvertently harasses her.

Your first step in correcting this type of misunderstanding is to make it clear to your child that his words and actions are meaningful and that other people do respond to them. Sometimes, children feel that their remarks and actions don't really count because they are rarely acknowledged or taken seriously by adults. If you feel this may be the case for your child, make a point of actively listening to what he says and let him know (in tactful ways) what your response is. Tell him, for example, "It hurts my feelings when you say I'm fat," or "I don't like to be pushed. It hurts. Please don't do that anymore."

Your next step is to pay attention to the specific words he uses and the way he acts when talking with friends and with adults. When you see that his actions are too overbearing—causing others to flinch or pull away—talk with him about this in calm, supportive ways, later when the two of you are alone. It's extremely important not to embarrass your child in front of others. If you see, or have received reports, that your child's jokes or comments cut too deep with his friends, talk with him about this, too—and make sure he is not picking up this habit from you.

Whether your child is a kindergartner just learning to get along with others or an adolescent uncertain how to approach a member of the opposite sex, offer him actual *scripts*, or conversational gambits, as well as examples of positive physical expression to help him adjust more easily. Before dropping your younger child off at a birthday party, try rehearsing some polite, age-appropriate remarks or questions. ("Thanks for inviting me," "You go first" or "No, thanks. I'm too full!") If you notice that he is having trouble sharing or dealing with conflicts at school, provide him with actual dialogue to solve these situations ("I'll give it to you in one minute, after I've finished" or "Okay, we'll play what you want, but then let's play what I want, okay?"). Your preadolescent or teenager may appreciate some discreet advice on how to let a girl know he likes her, how to get himself invited on an outing with a group he likes or how to politely remove himself from a relationship with someone he'd rather not spend time with.

IS IT HARASSMENT OR ROMANCE?

Many young people are unaware that what they say may be hurtful to others. Your child needs to learn to speak up when feeling uncomfortable and pay attention when others tell him that what he says or does is painful or makes them feel uncomfortable. Context is important here. If someone at school tells your adolescent daughter that she is "really beautiful," she might blush but feel flattered. Yet if the same remark is made to her twenty times a day by a boy she clearly dislikes, she may consider that harassment.

Your child can end most harassment by saying clearly and openly, "Please stop." She might need to follow up with more assertive statements, such as: "You know, when you do this, it doesn't make me like you," "What you say makes me feel creepy," or "I don't want to be near you." Point out to your child that being rude to or making fun of the aggressor may imply that she is "playing along." A put-down only begs for a response. She should state her position simply and honestly and then walk away.

If physical intimidation is involved, your child needs to ask adults for help, because there may be significant danger. If she says, "I can handle this," don't argue. Tell her which adults to turn to for help and what to say to them—and alert those adults that she may need their help. Your child may pretend not to be listening to this advice, but she really is, and it may be useful to her.

As your child grows, you will no doubt notice that he begins to adopt some of the little social quirks that you routinely use. If you tease your friends as a way of initiating a conversation, slap your spouse on the bottom as a sign of affection or interrupt others in your eagerness to get your point across, he may do the same. As you move through your days with your child, be aware of the lessons you are teaching him, and stick to the words and actions you hope he will use.

Bad Influences

We all know how difficult it is to change our habits. The task is all the more challenging when we lack support from those around us. You may find that your child simply cannot resist the social pressures at his school, in his neighborhood or even within his family. You can't always remove him from this unhelpful environment, but happily there are ways to mitigate its effects.

If you believe your child is being victimized or taught abusive behavior by his siblings or other relatives at home, don't leave him alone with them more than absolutely necessary. If he seems unable to escape a group of bullies at school, talk with his teachers and counselors about what you can do—both on your own and with your child. If he has fallen in with an abusive crowd in the neighborhood, he may be able to avoid them by participating in after-school and/or summer activities outside the immediate area. Your child's school counselor may be able to point you toward some appropriate resources that will provide your child and your entire family with help and support. Finally, you might want to consider moving your child to a new school or even moving the family to a new environment if that is possible. This is clearly a last resort. It is not only more convenient but a more positive solution to help your child triumph over bad influences wherever he happens to be.

Role Models

Again, it is important not only to actively combat negative or defeating elements in your child's life but also to point him in positive directions. You can find examples of positive social interaction for your child to follow in stories, films and the newspaper and among your family and friends. Be sure to remark on the good deeds and generosity that you observe in those you know—not in a way that reflects negatively on your child, but to let your child know what his family's true values are. As always, your own example will be the most powerful. By providing your child with clear rules, enforcing them consistently and fairly and interacting with others in considerate and thoughtful ways, you will provide him with the best environment in which to learn positive social behaviors that can improve his life.

CHAPTER EIGHT

TEAMWORK: TALKING WITH BULLIES AND THEIR PARENTS

"I DIDN'T KNOW RICHARD VERY WELL, but I'd known about him for years," recalled Carla, a parent speaking at an anti-bullying conference in Asheville, North Carolina. "His parents were hardworking immigrants—his mom worked three jobs and his father ran a restaurant, so they were never home. Richard used to wander the neighborhood by himself in all kinds of weather, even when he was little. He'd lose his house keys and be stuck out in the rain, and sooner or later one of us other parents would take him in for the afternoon.

"I felt sorry for Richard and encouraged my son, Zachary, to play with him even though Richard was a couple of years older. But then, when Richard was about thirteen and Zach eleven, a teenaged boy from another neighborhood became Richard's best friend. The two of them started ganging up on Zach—taunting him, excluding him from their games and finally stealing little things from Zach's room and from our house. Zach's dad and I told him not to play with them anymore, but Zach was mad about his stolen belongings. I suspect he continued to demand that they be returned.

"One afternoon, Zach came home crying, with a bloody nose and blood on the front of his shirt. Richard and his friend had ambushed Zach outside the playground and beaten him up pretty severely. I was stunned. Zach had never been in a fight before. I didn't know what to do. Should I find Richard and talk to him? Should I go see his parents? But they didn't speak English well, and I didn't know them. Still, I couldn't just do nothing. Richard lived on the route that Zach walked to school every day. We couldn't risk his being ambushed again.

"Finally, I called the police. They found Richard, spoke to him pretty roughly in my presence and let him go with a stern warning. Then, to my surprise, they took me to his mother's house and told her what had happened with me right there. This was very embarrassing to me. I hate confrontations and Richard's mother, who could barely understand what was happening, just kept murmuring, 'So sorry, so sorry,' and smiling timidly at me. Finally, we left.

"To be honest, I didn't expect anything to change. Richard was clearly turning out badly. With his parents at work all the time, how was he going to improve? But, to my relief, Richard avoided our whole family from that day on, even if he did toss me a resentful glance whenever we crossed paths. His teenaged friend—the one who had helped him beat up Zachary—stopped hanging around our neighborhood. Months later, I heard through the grapevine that Richard had changed schools. When I happened to spot him on the sidewalk, I thought he looked a little less lost, less angry, than he had when he was younger. Later, I heard he'd joined a church group and had a job at the grocery store.

"Then one day, about four years after the bullying incident, I was walking down the sidewalk and saw Richard coming my way. There was no way to avoid him, so I just kept walking. But he walked right up to me, looked me in the eye, and said, 'I'm sorry about what I did to your son that day. It was wrong. Can you forgive me?'

"I was very surprised, needless to say. I stammered something like 'Yes,' and he nodded and walked away. I guess this apology was part of some religious or recovery program he was involved in. But it meant a great deal to me. Looking back, I could see that that incident had made a big difference in all of our lives. I already knew that it had solidified the bond between Zach and us, because he saw that his family wouldn't stand for his being abused. But I saw now that, contrary to what I had assumed about Richard's mother, she had listened to what the police had told her and had made real changes in her son's life because of it. She had gotten rid of Richard's bullying friend, changed his school and taken the time, apparently, to get him thinking in moral or religious terms about his behavior.

"I am so glad now that those policemen took me to talk to her. I never would have done so on my own because of my assumptions about her and, I guess, my prejudices. But I was wrong. She was a good parent—just an overextended one. In spite of her personal problems, she took action on her son's behalf. And now Richard, whom no one in the neighborhood would have given two cents for ten years ago, is a young man with a good job, good friends and a decent future ahead of him."

"BUT I DON'T KNOW THEM"

These days, when it is quite common for children to interact even if their families don't know each other, the idea of confronting a bully or her parents can be a daunting prospect. If you are faced with a family of a different culture, ethnicity, economic level, religion or other identifying group, you may feel even more pessimistic about the possibility of working with them to solve the problem. You may fear that the bully and her parents will treat your concerns as inconsequential or amusing, or that they will respond to your objections by stepping up their aggressive behavior toward your child and even yourself. In some cases, you may suspect that the bully learned her aggressive behavior from an abusive parent and that talking to that parent will only lead to more abuse.

It is important to remember in such situations that your lack of knowledge about the aggressor's family cuts both ways—that is, they may be more concerned about their child's behavior than you realize. A child whose parents spend little time with her, as in the case of Richard described above, may simply be unaware that anything is wrong and welcome your intervention. A family whose culture doesn't place great emphasis on discouraging aggressiveness may still consider good manners and proper behavior quite important. Affluent parents may turn out to be concerned about the social responsibility such good fortune brings with it, and those who are less well off than you may appreciate your empathy, honest concern and practical help.

Much more important than the differences among families, in fact, are the similarities. Most parents passionately hope that their children will grow up to become positive, productive members of society. If your child is being harassed and has been unable to solve the problem on her own, you must intervene to protect her emotional health and safety. But you must also intervene for the sake of the other child. Approaching the aggressor and her family is not a matter of accusation and judgment—not a case of setting one family against another. Properly done, it is an approach to problem-solving that can bring families together and have an enormously positive effect on both children and their parents, and even on society as a whole.

IDENTIFYING THE PROBLEM

Whether you have only just now heard about a bullying problem or have been trying to help your child resolve one for some time, your first step, before approaching the bully or his family, is to get the facts straight. Carefully review the incident or series of incidents with your child, looking for clues to what caused the aggressive behavior and how it might be stopped. Ask your child who approached whom first, what exactly started the conflict, how she reacted to the harassment, whether the other child knew he was causing pain and continued anyway, and how the incident ended. Find out whether there were any witnesses, and whether any adults or children tried to intervene. Ask specific questions about the bully and his family that may help you understand why he behaved as he did (see box on page 145).

Hard as it can be to remain objective when you see that your child has been hurt, try to look at the situation as *a problem that needs solving*, not as a crime that must be prosecuted. Approaching this situation in anger or criticizing either party will only invite resistance from both your child and his attacker. Keep in mind that both parties are still children (even if they are adolescents), and that though we often use the word *bully*, an aggressive child may not be a thug. Bully, victim or bystander, all children are in need of adult guidance and support in these situations.

If your child is reluctant to divulge all the details of the incident, or you suspect he is not telling the entire truth, understand that this is perfectly natural for a child who fears a parent's reprisal or a bully's revenge. To get the information you need to approach the problem effectively, you may need to reassure your child several times—and demonstrate through your responses—that you do not intend to punish him, embarrass him or put him in greater danger than he was before. Sometimes, particularly with younger children, an indirect approach works best: a discussion about a book or TV show about bullying, an account of your own experience with bullying as a child, or a conversation about another child's victimization. If your child still resists, try to make another confidant available—

an older sibling, your child's other parent or another trusted adult. Make sure this person is present at times when your child is likely to feel like talking, such as on a long car ride or at bedtime.

You may find that, like many other parents in this situation, you will never know the whole story of what went on between your child and the aggressor. Your child may have what he considers a valid reason for withholding information (the bully may, for instance, have threatened to hurt his best friend or a family member if he "squealed"). In this case, there's no point in making him feel worse. It is possible to approach the bully while still holding some questions in reserve. In fact, since we can never know fully what happened during a bullying incident at which we were not present, withholding judgment is always a good idea.

SPEAKING WITH THE AGGRESSIVE CHILD

One of the reasons your child may withhold information about her harassment is because she wants more than anything for you *not* to interfere. Again, this is a natural response—we all prefer to solve our own problems, and no child wants others to think of her as a baby who can't take care of herself. However, if your child has tried without success to manage a bullying situation—or it involves physical or sexual abuse that puts her in serious danger—it is your duty as a parent to intervene in spite of her objections. You can soften the blow to her self-esteem, however, by representing your involvement as part of a "master-apprentice" process. Explain to her that you are stepping in this time to show her how confronting a bully can be accomplished successfully so that next time she can take a more active role herself. This approach may also help you to act more responsibly as you model calm, assertive behavior for her.

As your apprentice, your child will need to be informed ahead of time about what you plan to say or do. This is a good idea in any

WHAT YOU NEED TO KNOW ABOUT THE AGGRESSOR AND HER FAMILY

Before approaching anyone about an issue as complex and difficult as bullying, it is best to know as much as possible about their situation. If you do not know the child and are unfamiliar with her home situation, try to find out the following from your child, from the other child's teacher or from other adults who know her:

- Is this child known as a bully, or did something specific and unusual cause the incident?
- Does the child bully others as well, or is her aggression focused only on your child?
- Is the bully a ringleader or a follower? If she is a follower, who is she following?
- Has she been disciplined previously for bullying at school or elsewhere?
- How involved is the child's family in her daily life? Do they participate in school or neighborhood activities? Do their neighbors know them?
- Are the parents aware of their child's negative behavior? Have they acted in any way to correct it?
- Do the parents engage in any behavior themselves (emotional outbursts, criminal activity) that might encourage bullying tendencies in their child?
- Is the child bullied by her parents or older siblings?
- Is the family experiencing unusual stress or hardship?
- Does your child know the bully's parents? If so, what is your child's relationship with them?

case, since she may be able to provide valuable insight or criticism regarding your approach. She may, for example, point out that your plan to inform the bully that you will report his actions to his parents if he doesn't stop is pointless since the bully's parents are in the middle of a difficult divorce and he has little interaction with them. The more she can contribute to the process in this way and help you shape your plan, the more empowered she will feel and the more confident she will be that she can manage such a situation herself if it happens again.

Again, it is best to approach the bully calmly and nonjudgmentally, while clearly asserting your child's rights. There is no need to shout accusations or even to threaten the aggressor with reprisal at this point. Every child has rights—even a bully—and it is not your place to intimidate, frighten or punish anyone else's child. In most cases, a lengthy discussion is not necessary, either. Your child's aggressor is likely to catch on as soon as you:

- State the problem as you see it.
- Define the bad behavior.
- Tell the bully how his behavior affects your child.
- Ask him to stop it.
- Offer your help. Listen carefully to what he has to say.
- Remember to always put your own and your child's personal safety first when approaching anyone in a bullying situation.

If, for example, your child's best friend relentlessly teases her about her braces whenever other girls are around, calmly say to her, "Monique, you keep making fun of Julie for something she can't control. It's not right to make fun of people's appearance. It hurts her feelings and makes her think you're not really her friend. Would you please not do it anymore?" Then wait for a response. If the aggressor apologizes, accept the apology gracefully on your child's part and move quickly on to something else to spare her undue embarrassment. If she laughs or tries to minimize the problem, calmly repeat what you have said or casually ask any other kids who are present what they think about this situation—and then let peer pressure have its effect. In most cases, a little effort goes a long way with children who are bullying out of thoughtlessness rather than directed, intense rage.

By approaching the situation in this assertive but not aggressive manner, you have demonstrated to the bully that you are concerned for his welfare as well as your child's—while demonstrating to your child that it is not so hard to stop others' abuse. Your child may complain that she used the same approach, but that in her case the bully just laughed and ignored her. If so, remind her that, just as bullies always pick on people they perceive as less powerful than themselves, they are usually equally intimidated by those they consider more powerful. In this case, the bully simply recognized your authority as an adult and responded accordingly. This difference in intrinsic power—more than any inability on the victim's part to handle the situation—is the real reason why, in so many cases, parents must intervene.

Your child may prefer to talk to the bully herself in your presence. If you feel she is old enough and has the necessary skills, by all means allow her to do so. Again, the two of you can arrange for her apprenticeship in bully management according to her level of ability. She may ask you to arrange for a meeting at which you and the other child's parents—or you and her teacher or other adult—are present. She may simply wish to speak directly to the child while you are there to provide an authoritative presence and (silent) moral support. Again, encourage your child to follow the steps outlined above and resist the temptation to shout, accuse, strike out or otherwise express emotion in nonproductive ways. Be sure that once she has provided her side of the story, she waits for a response. The bully may stop his behavior or even apologize, or he may provide new information that you and your child had not considered before. If so, listen carefully. You may be able to use the information to arrive at a solution to the problem. If, for example, the bully claims that he took your child's bike because "she always rides it around the neighborhood, showing off," you and your child may decide to offer him a turn on the bike or even offer to give him your child's old one. A bully's side of the story may also provide you with new information about your child that can help you guide her toward more positive social interactions in the future.

Approaching the bully, rather than his parents, carries the advantage of keeping matters simple—avoiding some of the misunderstandings and repercussions that many parents fear will result from parent-to-parent contact. It is surprising how often a simple statement from the victim's mom, dad or older sibling will instantly arrest a particular form of harassment (if not change the bully's general mode of behavior). If you find that your attempt to solve the problem directly with the bully has been unsuccessful, however, it may be necessary to take the next step and discuss the issue with his family.

"LET'S SOLVE THIS TOGETHER": SPEAKING WITH THE BULLY'S PARENTS

No one likes to be the bearer of bad news. When the bad news concerns a child's behavior, and when you don't know the child's parents, the situation is even less appealing. Some experts feel that approaching parents directly may not be appropriate in such situations. They counsel victims' parents to talk instead to school officials and let these educators approach the aggressor and his family. When in doubt about your child's safety or your own, this may be the best approach. But in cases when you feel sufficiently comfortable doing so, approaching the parents of a bully in a calm, nonjudgmental, problem-solving way can be an effective method for stopping the behavior—and even positively changing the bully's life.

The key to this approach lies in good preparation and a determination to focus on solutions rather than blame. As you make your plan for talking to the other parents, resist the temptation to look at the situation as a case of "the good guys versus the bad guys" and instead think about how you and the other parents can resolve the issue in a satisfying and lasting way. To accomplish this, you will need to do more than just describe the incident and leave the bully's parents to deal with it on their own. You will need to give a clear and fair account of what happened, listen carefully to the parents' response, consider any suggestions that your own child contributed to the problem in some way, and continue to discuss the situation until you and the other parents have come to a joint decision on how to correct it.

Making Contact

Making the initial contact with another parent can be the most intimidating part of the process of working out a problem between the children. You may feel so upset about the bullying or so unsure of your ability to remain objective in a face-to-face meeting that you prefer to write a letter or e-mail to the other parents or have a telephone conversation. While each of these methods makes the initial contact easier (and any one of them may be better than no contact at all), a meeting in person is preferable because so much information is conveyed through body language, facial expressions and other nonverbal methods. A face-to-face meeting can include your children and their valuable input, which would be lost with a letter or phone call.

If you do decide to set up a meeting, keep your initial call to the other parents brief and upbeat and your tone of voice clearly positive. Don't get into the details of what has happened over the phone. Simply introduce yourself, identify whose child you're the parent of, and inform the parents that you would like to talk to them in person about something that has recently come up between the kids. Assure the parents that it's nothing dire (unless it is) and that you just want to discuss the issue directly with them so that you can all deal with it more fairly and effectively. (Reassuring the parents that their child is not in "big trouble" is especially important if you suspect he may be being abused. If this may be the case, take care you do not make things worse for that child. If you are concerned, ask the school for help first.) If the other parents are willing, try to arrange for the children to take part. Questions are bound to come up during your discussion that only the children can answer. In any case, the point is to help the children learn to get along, and that is best done if they participate in the process.

There is always the possibility that the parents will refuse to meet with you, laugh it off, deny that there's a problem or accuse your own child of causing the trouble. This is unlikely, however, except in some extreme cases—when a face-to-face meeting would probably not be successful, anyway. Most parents are sufficiently concerned about their children's behavior to agree to anyone's polite request to discuss it.

Once a meeting time and place have been arranged, inform your child about your plans and ask him to come along, if that is what has been agreed. Explain to him that the meeting will be short and focused on solutions, not accusations. Tell him he will not be left alone, either with the bully or with her parents. Again, it may help to present the situation in "apprentice" form—explaining in a supportive (not condescending) way that you will run this show so he can learn how to manage such a situation himself next time. Emphasize that you need his help in providing information and perhaps even suggesting solutions.

Keeping It Simple

As with the initial conversation, it's best to keep your meeting with the other parents short, positive and focused on the issue. Global statements ("Your child is always causing trouble at school"), accusations ("He's a bully who torments little kids!") and judgments ("He's no good, and I know why") have absolutely no place in this discussion. Before you arrive for the meeting, consider how uneasy and even fearful you would be if another parent had asked to speak with you about a "problem" with your child. A little empathy for your counterparts, and some effort to help them through this difficult situation, will go a long way in getting them to cooperate. Before the meeting begins, be sure to talk with your child as well about how hard this meeting will be for everyone; ask him to put himself in the others' place and imagine how they feel. Get his assurance that he will be as tactful as possible.

Again, one of the reasons you are meeting in person is to convey through facial expressions and body language that you are not a threat to the other family but that you require a solution to the problem. Take care, then, to use a tone of voice and gestures that put the other family at ease to the extent that this is possible. Shake hands, smile and, if you are hosting, offer everyone something to eat and drink. Then get right to the point.

First, present the problem to the parents (ideally with the children present) in as neutral a manner as possible, without drawing any conclusions. Don't say, for example, "Your Mitch has been beating up on my Don on the bus every day for four months now and this has got to stop!" Say, rather, "It's our understanding that Don and Mitch have been having some problems on the bus ride home from school. Don says Mitch has been hitting him, and he's come home with a torn shirt and some bruises on some days. He says he's talked to Mitch and the bus driver about this, but it hasn't stopped.

Do you know anything about this?" It may help, as you state the problem, to pretend you are telling a story about two fictional children. Thoughts of your own child being beaten up may be emotionally overwhelming.

People react to unpleasant news in different ways, so the other parents' initial response could be disbelief, outrage, fury at their child or even relieved laughter that the behavior wasn't worse. Let this first reaction slide and wait for a second, more thought-out response. Remember that your child is watching and you want to model a calm, assertive and effective attitude. Whatever response the parents finally do provide, demonstrate your willingness to explore the facts and discuss the situation with the children (just as you did earlier with your own child). Allow the other family all the time they need to digest this news. Once they have done so, ask how you might all come up with a solution.

Giving the other family the first opportunity to suggest ways to resolve the situation is a good idea because it allows them to escape the inevitable (and largely unproductive) feelings of shame and humiliation that arise from being confronted in this way. By offering one or more solutions, the bully and his parents escape their defensive position, and the meeting may therefore end more successfully. No matter how angry you are at the bully—and even, perhaps, at her parents—remind yourself that no one can positively change her behavior if she feels already judged and sentenced. Support and encourage any effort to face up to the problem and end the conflict. Empathize with the parents and share your own concerns as a parent. Don't be defensive. Listen to their side and act in a responsible way—the way you would like them to act.

A Positive Conclusion

If the bully and her parents insist on treating the situation as a threat, a joke or a nonissue, you may have no choice but to end the

RACE RELATIONS

No matter what race or religion you and your child are members of, you may feel uneasy if the family you are approaching about a bullying problem identifies with a different culture. When members of different groups get together to talk there is always the potential for misunderstanding, and the potential is much greater when the topic is the touchy issue of children's behavior. No one wants to believe his child is a bully or a victim—or even a bystander who did nothing to help. You will need to prepare for your conversation with special care. You can best do this by downplaying the us-versus-you element in this situation and focusing on how you can all work together to find a solution to what is a very common and understandable parenting problem.

Make a point, when speaking to parents about a problem with their child, to share your own concerns as a parent ("I don't always agree with everything my kid does—and I love him to death—but if he'd gotten involved with something like this I'd want to know, so I thought you might, too.") Emphasize the fact that you are relaying information about their child that you've heard about or witnessed to help them better understand him and support him. Be prepared, however, for at least some resistance at first as the other parents try to digest this unpleasant information. They may indeed question your motives or think you are being biased or discriminatory. They may even call you a racist, sexist or some other inflammatory term. Keep in mind that this response is a measure of the parents' concern, and in some cases their confusion—not necessarily a statement about you. If they tell you to mind your own business, repeat calmly that you are simply concerned about your child and had hoped the information you gave them would be helpful

(continued)

to everyone. If this does not go over well, give them a couple of days to think about what has happened and then try
to approach them again. Their initial reaction may have
been more a function of their surprise and confusion than of
any real, deep feelings they have. In some cases you may
not be able to breach the cultural and emotional barriers
that exist and must turn to "outside" authority figures—
school personnel, the police, an attorney, a counselor—
instead. See Chapters 9 and 10 for more information on
how to do this effectively.

meeting and seek redress elsewhere—from school officials, the police, the legal system or from other sources. If, however, they have
made any effort to meet you halfway, take advantage of their willingness to help solve the problem. Almost any proposed solution is
fine as long as it includes specific, agreed-on changes in behavior
and provisions concerning when and how to monitor the results.
The other parents may, for instance, insist that their child apologize
immediately for her behavior and elicit a promise from her not to
approach your child on the bus again. They may agree to talk with
you on the phone once every week or so for the next month—or to
check with the bus driver—to be sure that this promise is carried
out. You may match their effort with a promise to keep daily tabs on
your child's experience, to work with him on any provocative behavior he may have exhibited, and to contact the other parents right
away if you learn of any new problems with their child. While you
are unlikely to leave the meeting on the best of terms with these parents, your efforts to work together will almost certainly create a
much stronger and more positive environment for your children.
Bullying must not be tolerated, nor can it be ignored. By clearly and
assertively addressing this issue with parents, you have gone a long
way in improving your child's world and, perhaps, the other child's
future.

Following Up

Excellent as many parents' intentions are going into the process, they may stumble after the initial contact. It is important to follow up on your meeting with the bully and her parents—not only to ensure that the bullying has stopped but to fortify your working relationship with the parents and better the chances that the child has not simply targeted someone else or employed another form of harrassment. Maintaining communication with her parents—and with other parents and adults in your child's environment—makes it much harder for bullying to occur.

Following up also allows you to monitor to some degree the effect that your meeting has had on the other child. If you realize that as a result of your discussion with her parents, the child is being severely punished or abused (a rare occurrence, but it can happen), you must act on this suspicion by talking with the child or her parents or contacting the local Department of Social Services, an abuse hotline, a social service agency, appropriate religious counselor or even, if necessary, the police. Keep in mind that the bully is a child, just like your child. Like any child, she deserves the protection of every adult who knows her. In any case, her bullying is only likely to grow worse if she herself is being victimized.

Don't forget to follow up with your own child as well. Talk with him about the feelings he experienced before, during and after the meeting with the bully and her family. Ask him if he feels better now that all concerned parties have begun to address the problem. Ask him what he will do if he is ever bullied again in this or any other way. No matter what he tells you, support him in his efforts to work through this difficult situation, and let him know how proud you are of the courage and fortitude he has shown in facing up to this challenge.

IF YOUR CHILD IS THE AGGRESSOR

If you have been contacted by other parents regarding your child's behavior and have agreed to meet with them to discuss the issue, you are to be congratulated on your effort to do what is best for your child and everyone else involved. It is certainly difficult and sometimes even frightening to face such a situation, and often truly hard to believe that one's child is at fault. Even if you don't believe your child has bullied anyone, it is wise to take such complaints seriously. Even exaggerated claims can reveal the first signs of a developing problem that, if quickly and appropriately addressed, can be resolved before it creates serious difficulties. In the meantime, as you anticipate a meeting with the other child's parents, keep in mind the fact that they are no doubt uneasy thinking of how you will respond. Try to put your nonproductive emotions aside for now and instead focus on the problem and on ways in which it might be solved.

Your first response, once you have agreed to a meeting, is to ask your child what has been going on. Clearly, you will need to ask in as calm and nonjudgmental a way as possible if you are to elicit an honest and full response. As with a victimized child, a child accused of wrongdoing may be more inclined to confide in you if you recall a similar incident in your own childhood, tell or read a story about bullying and then talk about it with her, or use a bullying incident in a television show or film to start a conversation. As she lays out the details for you—or whatever portion of the incident she is willing to reveal—suspend judgment about her guilt or innocence. If she claims that the other child "asked for it" or "started it," simply nod and listen. If you feel she has not told you the whole story, let her know in a calm, nonthreatening way that you are going to talk with any other people you know who may have witnessed the incident to see if you can learn more. This may prompt your child to tell you more herself so that she can control the way the information is presented.

Just as it takes courage for you to face this situation with the victim's parents, so it takes a great deal of courage for your child to face you. Be sure to acknowledge this bravery in the face of what is clearly a difficult situation for her. If you feel that she may have been at fault, now is the time to begin talking supportively with her about precisely what she did wrong—expressing her annoyance by striking out, for example, instead of by avoiding the other child or reporting his behavior to an adult. Talk with your child about how she would feel if someone acted in the same way toward her. Ask her to suggest ways in which she might respond more appropriately next time. Remember, even if you don't believe that the action was as serious as the other child's parents made it out to be, talking about a minor incident now can prevent a great deal of trouble later on. Don't overreact to your child's unkind behavior, but don't discount it, either. Use this incident as a tool for helping her learn to interact with others in more positive ways.

Ideally, by the time the meeting with the other family actually occurs, you and your child will be prepared with an apology (if one is called for), an explanation (if one is required) and at least one or two ideas about how to address the situation. These suggestions are best provided by your child, since she will be the one to carry them out. The more actively she participates in this way in the resolution process, the more likely it is that she will learn something from the experience.

As the other family describes the problem, focus on listening carefully to what they say rather than formulating your child's defense. Do your best to make sure that your child is listening, too. After you've heard their complaint and discussed other pertinent matters, ask your child to apologize and propose her solutions. Again, concentrate on keeping the meeting short, simple and businesslike. Refrain from emotional outbursts. If your child finds it impossible to resist, ask her to leave the room until she has calmed down. Your aim is to correct behavior that is causing pain—not to cast blame or establish guilt or innocence. It is not necessary for every detail of the conflict to be rehashed or settled in any way— only for the two parties to agree on a way to proceed without future clashes.

Once you've reached an agreement on how the two children will behave toward each other in the future, thank the other family for making the effort to contact you and thank both children for participating. Assure the other parents that you will follow up on your child's promises and keep in touch with them—and be sure to keep these promises. Through your own example as well as your advice and guidance, you can demonstrate to your child the benefits of a positive attitude, careful communication and a commitment to getting along with others.

If it turns out that your child has indeed broken rules for which there are clear consequences in your family—if she has, for example, spread cruel rumors about another child even though saying mean things about others is against family rules—you must strictly enforce those limits. Aside from this, however, there is generally no need to extend the punishment unduly if your child is showing a sincere effort to understand why her behavior was wrong and to change it for the better. Except in the most extreme cases your firm, consistent enforcement of consequences, along with careful monitoring in the months to come, will change her behavior more effectively than emotional outbursts or severe punishment. While it is generally incorrect to assume that a child who has been bullying others is in need of a boost in self-esteem, it is true that children in this situation often benefit a great deal from an increase in focused, careful attention from their parents and other responsible adults.

IF TALKING DOESN'T WORK

Sadly, it is not always possible for families to talk a situation through and work together toward a solution. If your child has been accused of bullying and either denies everything despite the evidence or refuses to cooperate in changing his behavior, you may need to seek help from a counselor, religious advisor, social worker or therapist. In Chapter 10, we will discuss these and other options for parents who are concerned about their children's actions. Meanwhile, try not to judge your child or yourself too harshly. Children grow and learn and are capable of astonishing leaps in their understanding of the world. Your child can certainly gain from this experience if it leads to greater introspection.

Families of children who have been victimized are likely to feel doubly disappointed if a meeting with the other family fails to bring about positive results—first because the bullying behavior has not been corrected and second because the victim has failed to see how such a situation can be resolved positively. If you find yourself in this position and are aware that the other child's parents are not seeking further help for their child, you may need to turn to your child's teachers or other school personnel, or even to your local police force or other adults in the community. In Chapters 9 and 10 you will find direction on making use of these resources, as well as obtaining orders of protection, filing civil suits and seeking other forms of legal redress.

Some parents have been so moved by their children's experiences with bullying that they have organized victims' support groups or anti-bullying campaigns in their communities. They have written letters to the editor, lobbied the media for more attention on the issue and even supported the enactment of state laws protecting children from bullying and other forms of abuse in public places and elsewhere. It is quite moving to see the profound emotion that is expressed at gatherings of victimized children and their families, as well as the support they receive from neighbors and acquaintances who may not have been victimized but have witnessed such abuse. If you and your child have not found a solution with this particular aggressor, consider the possibility of finding much greater fulfillment—by creating a space in which all children can find solace, advice and inspiration from others who have endured the same type of experience and not only survived but thrived.

CHAPTER NINE

INTERVENING
AT SCHOOL

ROB REMEMBERS ALL TOO CLEARLY how cruelly he was bullied in high school. He was singled out as a victim for reasons he still can't articulate. When he turned to his teachers for help, he found out that they were of little use. "It was like they felt helpless, too," he told me. "They were scared of the bullies and didn't want to draw attention to themselves." A top student, Rob lost his confidence and his enthusiasm for school to such an extent that he dropped out at age sixteen. Though he eventually completed his education, the years of bullying left a great deal of emotional damage in their wake.

When I met Rob, his eldest daughter, Serena, had just turned thirteen. The previous year, she had confessed to her father that a group of other girls at her middle school were spreading cruel rumors about her, taunting her on campus and playing practical jokes on her in the lunchroom. "I am so glad she came to me," he said. "I knew how it felt and I wasn't going to let it happen to my child. I made an appointment with Serena's counselor and took her with me to the meeting. Her counselor and teachers tried to brush the inci-

dents off, but I wouldn't let them. I told them harassment is a serious issue that can cause real psychological harm, and I said I would
not send my daughter back to the school until some kind of effective
action was taken."

Rob's prompt response and assertive follow-up eventually led to
the bullying ringleader's suspension, along with an agreement from
school officials to keep an unobtrusive eye on his daughter to ensure
that the bullying did not continue. When several of the bullies
threatened his daughter with violence because she had "told," she
reported their threats to school officials and provided corrobora-
tion from witnesses. Those girls were suspended as well. Single-
handedly, in other words, Rob had begun to change the social
climate of his daughter's school. Every student in the school benefited as a result. "My daughter isn't bullied anymore," he told me.
"Those kids who were mean to her are still there, but they leave her
alone. She's making good grades and she's a happier, healthier kid. If
only more parents would take bullying seriously, and make sure
school employees pay attention to the issue, we could make incredible improvements in our kids' lives."

"THEY NEVER LISTEN"

We all carry with us memories—both good and bad—of our experiences at school. When our children come home with stories of
being teased, beaten up, sexually harassed or taunted on school
grounds, we cannot help but relive unresolved feelings of mortifica-
tion, rage, guilt and frustration. The thought of having to turn
again to teachers, counselors and other school officials for help can
seem overwhelming at first—particularly if we received little or no
help from them when we were students. We may wonder if the
teachers view our children as "typical victims" or "complainers" and
if they will think the same about us. While these are all perfectly

normal reactions to have, it would be a terrible shame to allow them to get in the way of ensuring our children's safety.

The fact is, most educators loathe bullying at least as much as parents and children do. They have witnessed firsthand, year after year, what bullying does to the spirit, performance and health of a victimized child. What teachers and other educators need is a clear mandate and support from parents to eradicate bullying *on a school-wide basis.* Students must be educated about bullying's effects and how to respond to it; bullying must not be tolerated by adults on campus, on school buses or at the bus stop; and bullying behavior must consistently meet with negative nonhostile, nonphysical consequences whenever it occurs. As many important studies have demonstrated, this type of organized, concerted effort to change the social climate of the school leads to measurable improvements not only in student safety but in academic performance, school morale, school attendance and behavior in general.

In this chapter, I will present the steps to take in instituting an anti-bullying campaign or otherwise working toward a restructuring of the social environment at your child's school. You don't need to dedicate yourself full-time to this effort or to make sweeping changes on your own in order to help your child. As we saw in Rob's case, a brief series of conferences with teachers, counselors or other school officials may be all it takes to turn the tide. The good news is that, in the wake of the shooting incidents that have occurred at various schools across the country, school personnel are generally much more sensitized to the issue of bullying than they were when you were in school, or even five or ten years ago. You may be surprised at how eagerly educators welcome your suggestions and how willing they are to work with you in solving your child's problem and addressing the issue of bullying at school.

In the end, of course, it does not matter whether your child's teachers are initially open to your efforts or not. As the institution charged with the care and education of your child, the school and its employees are responsible for his health and safety while he is on school grounds. Nevertheless, you are likely to meet with positive results faster if you approach teachers and other officials with a positive attitude, solicit their ideas and observations and express your willingness to work with them—not just to protect your child but to improve life for everyone on campus.

TALKING WITH YOUR CHILD'S TEACHER

"I *did* tell the teacher, Mom! He doesn't care. Jerry's always pulling up girls' skirts in class and trying to look down their blouses. Mr. Hanford just looks the other way and pretends he doesn't see." Few parents make it all the way through their children's school years without hearing some comment along these lines. Some such complaints may be exaggerated (Jerry doesn't *always* harass the girls, or Mr. Hanford makes him stop when he *notices*). Nevertheless, there may come a time when your child is experiencing bullying at school to such a degree that she needs your help. It is true that, in many cases, teachers do not notice bullying even when it occurs in their classrooms. Bullies do their best to harass their victims when and where adults can't see them, and there are any number of things going on in a typical classroom that require a teacher's attention. Still, all teachers are aware that bullying occurs. Even a teacher who might prefer to ignore a bullying problem will usually pay more attention if a parent demonstrates his concern.

When you make an appointment with your child's teacher, explain briefly and calmly what the meeting will be about and ask whether it's all right to bring your child along. Most teachers will want the child present to provide necessary information and clarify any misunderstandings. It is good for your child, too, to participate as actively as possible in the problem solving. You may find it help-

ful to review the incident or series of incidents with your child before the meeting, writing down exactly what happened (i.e., when
and where it happened and the names of those who witnessed the
event). This information will not be used to "prosecute your case"
but to provide concrete information to the teacher. It may also save
time at the meeting—an act of consideration your child's teacher
may appreciate.

Be sure to begin the meeting—and to see that your child begins—
with a positive attitude. No matter what your child has told you
about the teacher's unwillingness to deal with bullying in his classroom, give him the benefit of the doubt until and unless he proves
you wrong. As the central adult in your child's school day, this
teacher holds sway over a great deal of her experience. He may be
more willing to focus on easing her discomfort in his classroom if
you demonstrate that you appreciate his efforts and are open to
working together as a team. Keep in mind, too, that your child is observing your approach and will learn from your example how best to
interact with authority figures.

Your first duty at this meeting is to calmly present the facts as
your child has reported them in clear, chronological order. If your
child has attempted to stop the bullying on her own, or you have
met with the other child's parents to discuss the issue, describe these
attempts and the actions that resulted. If your child believes the
bully abused her on another child's orders or for a specific reason,
offer these reasons as possibilities to consider. If there were witnesses to the abuse, provide the names of these children (or adults).
It's a good idea to present this information in written form if there is
more of it than the teacher could easily recall later.

Once you have stated the facts, compare notes with the teacher.
Did he witness any of what your child described, was he aware of
what had occurred, or has he observed the aggressor treating other
classmates in similar ways? No matter how blatant the acts appear

to you and your child, it is quite possible that the teacher missed them. He is probably at least somewhat aware of who the bullies are in his class (a typical classroom contains three to five habitual bullies), but may be less conscious of which children are being victimized. A middle school or high school teacher who does not teach the same group of students all day may be completely oblivious to the social dynamics in his class. Ask him (neutrally, not accusingly) whether he has observed your child's behavior in his classroom and noticed she is in distress.

Your child's teacher may be able to provide you and your child with new observations and insight that will help you better understand and resolve the situation. He may be more familiar with the other child and his family than you and your child are, in which case he may inform you that the child is under unusual stress or that he has attempted to work with the child on similar problems before. He may even suggest behaviors he has observed in your own child— conscious or unconscious, deliberate or not—that allow the abuse to continue. Your child may, for example, continue to sit next to the bully in class or linger near him after the bell rings even though her proximity inevitably leads to taunts, retorts and shouting matches. (If your child or her teacher is uncomfortable having your child in the room while discussing these issues, respect his wishes and ask your child to wait outside the room. It is more important for you to have a thorough understanding of what's happening than it is for your child to be present throughout the meeting.) Whether or not you agree with the teacher's observations or consider them relevant, treat them as what they are: a sign that the teacher is engaged, willing to discuss and perhaps act on this problem. If the teacher discounts your child's report or can add no observations of his own, at least ask for his cooperation in developing a strategy to stop the bullying and monitor the outcome.

Creating Strategies

Ideally, you, your child and the teacher will all contribute ideas on how to solve your child's problem as quickly as possible. Be open-minded as you share and discuss ideas, then decide by consensus which to implement. The teacher may agree to assign seats in the classroom, for example, placing your child on the opposite side of the room from her aggressor. He may volunteer to work with the other child, and perhaps his parents, to change his behavior. Your child may agree to actively avoid the other child when given the choice and to report any further abuse immediately to her teacher. Finally, you can promise to follow up on this agreement, checking regularly with your daughter to be sure the plan is working and calling the teacher on a prearranged date to review the strategy and make changes if necessary.

Once the three of you have agreed to work together as a team, take a moment to talk with the teacher about the general climate that currently exists at the school regarding bullying. It is important to ask these questions in a positive, not a critical, way. Your aim is to get the teacher thinking about other ways to combat bullying on the school campus—not to put him on the defensive. Try asking:

- Are children educated about correct and unacceptable social behavior?
- Are there ever classroom discussions about such bullying-related issues as taking turns, respecting others' rights, letting another person know if he has hurt one's feelings and practicing the golden rule?
- How do you know these conversations aren't going over their heads?
- My understanding is that bullying often happens on playgrounds and in lunchrooms, bathrooms and

other "bullying zones." Are those places monitored
carefully by adults at this school?

If he responds agreeably, you might also talk with him about the
possibility of allowing his students to hold a class discussion about
bullying or even start an anti-bullying campaign. Point out that
when the entire class or student body agrees not to tolerate the behavior, the number of incidents quickly diminishes, since a bully
without an appreciative audience quickly loses interest in abusing
others. As we will see later in this chapter, organized programs frequently begin with just this type of informal parent-teacher conversation. Your enthusiasm and the teacher's can be enough to start the
process at your child's school.

Finally, be sure to inform the school principal and any other
school officials about the problem your child is experiencing and
the plan you and her teacher have made to address it. When dealing with schools, keep in mind that the principal is in charge and
needs to know what is going on. Offer to help the principal in whatever way you can to see that your child is protected while under the
school's care.

MOVING UP THE LADDER:
YOUR CHILD'S COUNSELOR, SCHOOL
PRINCIPAL AND OTHER ADMINISTRATORS

There are many reasons to take your child's problem with a bully to
a school counselor, the principal or other responsible personnel.
Your child's teacher may have been unable or unwilling to stop the
bully's behavior, or the bully may be in a different grade, classroom
or even school. The bullying may be taking place on the school bus
or during an after-school session or other place where her teacher
has limited or no jurisdiction. You may wish to discuss the problem
with several different teachers or with the bully and his family; a

---

THE OTHER ADULTS IN YOUR CHILD'S LIFE

Due to the constant presence of a watchful teacher, the classroom is actually one of the less popular venues for bullying. Your child is likely to encounter more serious conflict in the lunchroom, on the playground, in the gym or locker room, at the bus stop and on the bus. If your child has been bullied in any of these places, it is still important to discuss the problem with her teacher as well as the adult responsible for monitoring the scene of the event. The teacher or school administrator can confer with playground supervisors, lunchroom monitors, coaches and club advisors to create an effective strategy to protect your child. Bus drivers, after-school teachers and other responsible adults need to know that other school personnel are aware of what has been happening and are monitoring your child's welfare.

Your child's teacher can also use the information you have given him to understand and deal with any drop in grades, truancy, temporary depression or other reaction your child experiences as a result of her experience. Whether or not your child is suffering in the classroom, the presence of an adult ally in this central location is bound to improve her day.

---

principal's or counselor's office is often the best place for this. You may feel more comfortable with one of these administrators than you do with your child's teacher and may decide for this perfectly valid reason to take your child's problem to them.

Whomever you approach, it is once again best to bring your child with you and important to enter the meeting with a positive, team-oriented attitude. Upset as you may be about your child's experience, you will find that others can more efficiently help you if you keep your emotions under control. Don't forget to bring notes you have taken on your child's initial experience, any attempts to resolve the situation and any conversations you or your child have had with the bully, his parents, your child's teacher and any witnesses to the event. The more clearly and simply you can present the facts, the sooner you and the school official can find a solution.

If your child is emotionally overwrought from her bullying experience, a school counselor, school psychologist or school social worker can be a wise choice of an ally. These professionals are, overall (and especially in recent years), quite sensitive to the issue of bullying and fully aware of the damage it can cause. They can not only help you work out a solution to your child's problem in practical ways but can also talk privately with her about any anxiety or depression she feels and counsel the aggressor about his inappropriate behavior. They can arrange for a meeting between families at which they act as moderator, mediate between bully and victim or arrange for fellow students to do so, and may talk with you about how you might begin to accept and learn from this experience. They can also refer either or both children to other programs or services that may help them recover and even thrive.

Unfortunately, not all schools provide counseling services or mental health professionals. You may find that at your child's school the vice principal or principal performs a similar service. Usually, these officials focus more on functional ways to correct the situation—getting all involved parties together for a talk, punishing the bully or changing class schedules. You may feel that this approach better suits your child's personality or situation, or you may choose to speak with one of these administrators because of their power to see that other school employees (such as bus drivers and playground monitors) effectively ensure students' safety.

Even if you have spoken with your child's teacher and feel that her problem is being resolved successfully, it can't hurt to request a brief meeting with the school counselor and administrator as well. The more adults who are aware of your child's situation and looking out for her, the better—and if you have filled them in ahead of time, you will be able to call on them instantly in time of need.

In larger schools or those that are less open to meeting with parents, you may find that school personnel listen politely as you describe your child's problem but never take action to solve it. In this case, you may need to make a somewhat more dramatic gesture to focus attention on your child's needs. One mother who got no response to her reports that her son was repeatedly beaten up in the school bathroom finally asked for permission to install a video camera near the sinks. When she was able to show the school principal a videotape of half a dozen boys being robbed of their lunch money in the bathroom, one after another, the principal promised to hire a monitor for every bathroom during school hours. This parent was careful to follow up on the promise—making sure that the monitors were hired before the end of the semester break. You, too, may need to visit or telephone several times to review the progress of the school's anti-bullying strategy and encourage change if necessary.

If change is still slow in coming, don't hesitate to bring this issue up at school board meetings or PTA meetings. Some parents have even been inspired to run for a position on the school board themselves in order to address the problem of bullying and violence at their children's schools. The schools—and the students—have benefited as a result.

ZERO TOLERANCE: WHAT CAN SCHOOLS DO?

In the wake of the recent mass shootings and other violent incidents at United States schools, education officials have attempted to ensure students' safety in a variety of ways. Some schools search backpacks, use metal detectors and rely on armed guards to patrol school corridors. One of the most effective methods for controlling school

KEEP RECORDS AND DON'T GIVE UP

In an ideal world, all teachers, administrators and other school officials would have the time, energy and resources to focus on each and every student—protecting, nurturing and educating that child. Unfortunately, the world isn't perfect and neither are our school systems. In the end, no one is ever going to care as much about your child's welfare as you do. Consider it your responsibility to keep track of what is happening in your child's social world. As you take steps to change a bad situation, keep careful written records of what happened, how your child responded, what actions were taken as a result and what was discussed at every meeting with the bully, his family and friends and with the school or other personnel. In most cases, your notes will help clarify what has happened and keep things reasonably objective. Worst case, you will need this documentation if you find yourself making a complaint against a school employee or filing a civil suit against the bully.

Your notes can also help you organize your own effort to improve your child's situation—by providing you with a timeline for reviewing her progress and a record of whom to call, visit or otherwise follow up with at the appropriate times. As your child, her teacher and others see how committed you are to solving this problem, they are more likely to make the effort to help. As a parent, you may not be able to count on school personnel to solve a bullying problem on their own, but you can certainly inspire them, help organize their thinking and then follow up repeatedly.

violence and other forms of cruelty is often spearheaded by parents, school mental health professionals and teachers concerned about student welfare. This method is the institution of a schoolwide intervention program aimed at educating children about bullying and its effects and restructuring the social environment so that bullying is no longer accepted at the school.

These intervention programs—with such names as "No More Bullying," "The Bullying Project," "Peace by Piece," "Dare to Care" and "Bully-Proof Your School"—share a number of common features and are similarly effective. When successfully instituted in the school as a whole, they have been shown to create:

- marked reductions in both direct and indirect bullying incidents
- reductions in other negative behaviors not related to bullying, such as vandalism, theft and truancy
- a more positive attitude toward social relationships, academic work and the school itself
- increased student satisfaction with school life
- no increase in bullying in other venues away from the school.

Dan Olweus, the expert in childhood aggression who designed the prototype on which many current programs are modeled, and whose research on the effects of such programs continues to influence educators today, has established certain key principles that must be a part of any such initiative. These include:

- the creation of a school environment characterized by warmth, positive interest and involvement from adults
- sufficient monitoring and surveillance of the students' activities in and out of school
- firm limits to unacceptable behavior
- nonhostile, non-corporal punishment when limits are violated.

The first step in instituting such a program involves educating students and adults about the types of bullying that occur at school and elsewhere, its effects and the most effective ways to respond to it. Usually, students are given surveys or questionnaires to fill out that focus on awareness and tolerance of bullying in school. Administrators then stage a schoolwide conference to introduce the program and inform students about the principles behind the program, the rules that will be enforced schoolwide, and the changes students will observe in how school personnel monitor student behavior and intervene when bullying occurs. Shortly afterwards, classes meet to discuss the issue more freely and to institute class rules against bullying. Teachers may choose to introduce structured curricula that explore the causes and implications of aggression. (In many cases, teachers have received workshop training in how to present these topics.) Meanwhile, playgrounds, bathrooms, lunchrooms and other bullying venues are monitored more closely. Bullies and victims are referred to a counselor or teacher for individual counseling and mediation, and bullying behavior is routinely punished without resorting to corporal punishment or other "bullying" methods. Counselors or school psychologists may also work with teachers and parents who are having problems with a bullying or victimized student.

The program is usually run by existing school staff members— usually school mental health professionals or perhaps the vice principal or school resource officer. Parents frequently serve as additional coordinators and monitors, and also meet to discuss the many issues raised during the day-to-day management of the program. In some cases, students are invited to participate in the planning and execution of the program as well. The coordinators frequently make an effort to heighten public awareness of bullying in the greater community, and the efforts sometimes inspire the creation of separate anti-bullying campaigns in churches and community groups.

As a consequence of these efforts, student awareness of bullying and its effects increases enormously, and tolerance for bullying behaviors plunges. Bullying is no longer seen as "funny" or "cool," and students are much more likely to help and support a victim than they might have been before. Through class discussions and counseling sessions, students also learn a great deal about the dynamics of aggression and the importance of addressing problems before they grow worse. They learn a wide variety of coping techniques to help them in times of conflict or miscommunication. These may include accepting compromise, saying no tactfully, expressing anger in acceptable ways and learning to move away or change activities when one feels emotionally or socially strained. As Dan Olweus has demonstrated, the frequency of bully/victim problems can decrease as a result by approximately 50 to 70 percent over the course of two years. As an added benefit, other antisocial behaviors such as van-

THE POWER OF THE PTA

As this section has demonstrated, parents who work together can create powerful, positive changes in their children's school environment. If you are concerned about the level of violence and cruelty your child encounters on a daily basis, consider how you might change her experience for the better. In the Resources section at the end of this book, you will find on-line and other sources of information for parents who wish to start a school-based anti-bullying campaign. If you don't feel up to creating a program from scratch, try introducing the subject of bullying at the next PTA meeting. Nearly all parents have had some experience with bullying, either in their own childhood or in the course of raising their kids. Most will be not only open but also eager to make the necessary effort to safeguard their children and to educate them in how to get along with others at school and elsewhere.

dalism, theft, drunkenness and truancy are likely to drop substantially and student morale improves. Clearly, learning social skills not only helps children solve immediate problems but also helps create a better community environment as well.

IF YOUR CHILD IS THE AGGRESSOR

"I think the day I got that phone call from the dean of students was probably the most embarrassing day of my life," Stan, a close friend, told me. "I had no idea Lucas was involved with a group of bullying kids. Nothing in my whole experience with him could have prepared me for the fact that he was scaring little kids out of their allowances and lunch money."

Stan had a hard time just talking about it. When explaining what happened, his face turned somber and his eyes teared up. "I went in to talk to the dean," he said, "and Lucas was there. He was so ashamed. He took one look at me and started crying." But as it turned out, Stan added, "That conversation with the dean was a turning point for us. She told me she believed that Lucas had a drinking problem, and that both the drinking and the picking on little kids were a result of his hanging out with a gang of kids who were more powerful than he was. She suggested I limit his social life and monitor his activities more closely. She recommended a counselor he could go see. Over the next few months, he and I had an incredible series of talks. He was a lot more upset over my job loss and our move to a new city than I realized. He'd lost his friends, left his old familiar neighborhood behind and didn't fit in in the new place. I was so busy looking for work I didn't notice how lonely he was. I don't know—if it hadn't been for that call from the school, he'd be in a lot worse shape than he is today."

You, too, may feel ashamed or angry if and when a teacher or school official informs you that your child has been involved in bullying behavior. Chances are that your child feels even worse. Such feelings are normal, given the situation, but as you arrange to meet with the representative at the school try to approach the situation positively. Remind yourself that children grow and change, and that all of them make mistakes in the process. If your meeting at school reveals a problem that can be addressed before it grows worse, count yourself lucky that your child's teachers and counselors care enough to intervene.

Once you have agreed to attend a meeting at the school, ask permission to bring your child with you so that he can contribute information and answer any questions. Next, ask your child—calmly and in a neutral tone—for his side of the story. Write down the facts so you can review them later in a less emotional frame of mind. At the meeting, you will also want to write down what the school official tells you about the bullying incident and your child's general behavior.

It may be helpful to remember that school officials, like all who take pride in their job, do not like failure. Their desire—to see your child excel and thrive—is identical to yours. Keep this in mind as you strive to talk in positive ways with your child's teacher or counselor about how you and the school can work together to resolve the problem. Listen carefully to the teacher's suggestions and try to follow them if you can. If you feel they are unreasonable or inappropriate, respectfully present an alternate solution.

Your child may or may not cooperate in this process. If he is willing to apologize for his behavior, accept the consequences, and change his habits, consider half the battle won. If he resists discussion of the situation and refuses to change his actions, you may find it necessary to provide him with a trustworthy, well-informed adult friend, religious counselor or therapist to help him through this period. Family therapy to improve communication at home may also make an enormous difference in all of your lives.

Finally don't forget to look at your own behavior. Are you asking your child to do something you wouldn't do (like apologize or change)? Is your punishment aggressive, threatening or punitive? If so, consider offering to make a change yourself to support the changes that you are asking your child to make.

IS IT TIME TO LEAVE?
IF YOUR SCHOOL DOESN'T RESPOND

Much as schools have improved their response to bullying among students, there are times when there's a bad fit between your child and the school. Sometimes children are unable to thrive despite their parents', teachers' and their own best efforts. While it is best for children to learn to manage and overcome bullying wherever they happen to encounter it, a child who continues to suffer may find welcome relief through a move to a new school or neighborhood. Such a move has no doubt saved the lives of a substantial number of children in extreme distress.

Before making this decision, take the time to research your options and choose a school that is clearly better suited to your child. If she is moving to a new school district, make sure that her new school takes bullying seriously and can provide her with support and counseling. Insist that she tour or visit private or parochial schools ahead of time so she can decide whether she would be comfortable there. If you suspect that bullying issues may resurface in the new setting (if you worry that your child will face more taunting, or will be tempted to start bullying again), consider the possibility of discussing this with her future teacher or counselor. Even if you decide not to mention your child's past problems specifically, arranging a meeting is an excellent way to establish a line of communication with the school and to encourage adult involvement in your child's school career.

You will also need to prepare your child for a new start. If she is willing, talk with her about her hopes and plans for this switch, and do what you can to support these goals. If you think she may benefit from counseling, therapy or a support group, this is a good time to provide it. She may simply wish to discuss her previous experiences with you or another trusted family member or advisor. Think carefully about ways she can change the social dynamic this time around. At the new school, where she has not already been labeled, she may be able to reimplement techniques—such as involving herself in a particular hobby or refining her social skills—that failed initially.

Where you relocate depends largely on her needs and your family's resources. Simply moving to another school can work in cases when your child's problems stem from a single relationship or serendipitous labeling. However, if the causes of your child's victimization travel with her—if she belongs to a victimized ethnic group or sexual persuasion, for example, or her self-esteem is low and her social skills are weak—she is likely to experience the same rejection again and feel doubly disappointed and depressed. A better choice in this case may be an alternative school designed specifically for such children, such as the Harvey Milk High School for lesbian and gay youth in New York City; a parochial or private school for children of a particular religion, ethnicity or gender; or any of the hundreds of alternative schools for children who don't feel comfortable in traditional public school environments.

If you are unable to find a school that's appropriate for your child's needs, you may want to consider starting a charter school. Charter schools are nonsectarian public schools founded for a specific purpose or to serve a specific population. They operate free of many of the rules and regulations that apply to other public schools, but are held accountable to their sponsors—usually a local school board—for academic performance and other educational standards.

Charter school classes are generally smaller than public school classes and they often practice innovative approaches to the standard curriculum. Charter schools can be founded by grassroots organizations consisting of parents, teachers and community leaders, local business leaders or the staff of an existing school. Clearly, founding such a school represents a major commitment, but it can reap big rewards for the parents and children who are willing to invest the time and energy. Smaller classes that allow for extra attention from teachers may be just what your child needs to succeed.

Homeschooling

Recently, an increasing number of parents have turned to homeschooling as a solution for children who are unhappy in the public school system. Nearly 800,000 children from ages six to seventeen were being homeschooled in 1999, and the numbers continue to grow. A rich supply of information and resources—including packaged curricula—is now available on-line to families who decide to continue their children's education at home (see Resources, page 211). Again, isolating your child from a problem such as bullying at school is not usually a long-term solution. Teaching her face-to-face social skills, problem-solving strategies and the ability to listen is essential to help ease adjustment and citizenship. Still, a child who has been severely challenged by her school experience may benefit from a temporary or even permanent leave of absence.

Before deciding to switch from a school to homeschooling, be sure to consider whether you and your child are really suited for this type of education. Your child needs to understand that homeschooling is not equivalent to "dropping out" or taking a vacation. She will need to continue to study and to expand her understanding in many areas. She will also be spending a substantial part of each day working alone with you. Ask her to consider these facts on her own and discuss them with you before she weighs in on the homeschool idea.

You must also ask yourself some serious questions about your ability to teach your child. Can you afford to do so—both in terms of forgoing paid work in order to teach your child and of purchasing the teaching tools you will need? Do you have the time to set aside for regular, daily, one-on-one attention to your child? Do you feel sufficiently well educated yourself to teach your child at her optimal level? Do you enjoy spending most of every day with your child, or do you need time by yourself? Are you self-disciplined enough to stick to a homeschooling schedule and your curriculum (if you have one)? Is your spouse willing to cooperate? A partner's support is important in getting homeschooling off to a good start.

Whatever academic environment you and your child decide to embrace, it's important to focus on the positive potential that this change represents, rather than the events that led up to it. Eventually, with care and attention, your child will learn to function well without being victimized wherever she finds herself in the world. For now, help her take advantage of this "time-out" to work on the issues that led to bullying in the past, change what she can about her own behavior to avoid problems in the future, and build her emotional and social strength for more successful relationships with others.

CHAPTER TEN

SEEKING PROFESSIONAL AND COMMUNITY HELP

ELEANOR KNEW SOMETHING was going on with her twelve-year-old son, Jason. For some time he had seemed listless and depressed. He had lost interest in his appearance and, over the course of the school year, his grades had plummeted. She ascribed some of these changes to adolescence and his move to middle school—but Jason seemed much more "lost" than other neighborhood boys his age and didn't seem to enjoy such benefits of teenaged life as plenty of friends and an active social life. He spent long hours alone in his room playing video games and listening to what Eleanor thought was disturbing music.

Eleanor tried several times to talk with Jason about what was wrong, but he shrugged off her advances. Busy with her own work life and her other children, Eleanor left it at that. By the end of the school year she had almost grown used to the new Jason. It came as an utter shock when, alone in the house one afternoon, her son committed suicide by swallowing several dozen sleeping pills.

"I wish every morning, noon and night that I had paid more attention to his distress," Eleanor says now. "It turned out that Jason was being sexually abused by an older boy in his youth group. I see now that he was isolated and completely confused. He had no one to talk with—no one to help him escape the abusive situation and work out the problems it was creating. If I had only gotten therapy for him in time and had that older boy arrested, Jason might be alive today."

"IF ONLY WE'D KNOWN"

Scenarios such as this one are every parent's worst nightmare, but the fact is that many children are lost each year because they lack knowledgeable help and support in a crisis. Children and adolescents who are chronically victimized may succumb to depression, drug abuse, self-abuse, suicide or episodes of violence against others. Those who experience severe trouble controlling aggressive impulses frequently begin to engage in drug and alcohol abuse, extreme violence and other criminal activity without professional intervention. Yet it can be difficult for a parent to tell the difference between behavior that is within the normal range and behavior that signals a need for professional help.

In this chapter, we will explore a number of situations that may require intervention by police, the legal system, professional counselors or therapists, the community at large or even, in some cases, the government. I will discuss signs to look for when deciding whether such attention may be necessary or helpful and examine the benefits and limitations of each type of response. In the end, there is no definitive answer to the question "Does my child need professional help?" Careful observation can, however, give you a good idea of whether your child's current efforts to deal with bullying behavior are working or whether she needs more immediate and long-term support.

"SHOULD WE CALL THE POLICE?"

Bullying occurs wherever children and adolescents congregate— not only on school grounds but also in the neighborhood, at sports events, in dance halls, on the beach, at public swimming pools, in parks and in private homes. Relatively minor taunting or rough-housing in any of these settings can quickly explode into real harassment and even physical or sexual violence. Clearly, if your child is subjected to a violent attack, rape or other form of criminal abuse, you must contact the police immediately. The aggressor must be sequestered before he hurts someone else, and your child must be physically protected. Your child also needs to see that there are clear, speedy consequences for such behavior and that he does not have to endure it.

Slightly less damaging situations can actually be more difficult for parents to manage, since they may not be sure whether police intervention would be helpful. If a bully gives your child a bloody nose, follows him down the street tossing sexual taunts and innuendoes or threatens to beat him up but has not actually done so, you may worry that calling the police is an overreaction that will backfire if the bully seeks revenge (or her parents respond in anger). In these cases, it may help to ask yourself the following questions:

• **Has the bully committed a crime?** A criminal act is always a reason to call the police. Repeated, credible threats of violence, slanderous statements on school or other public property, theft and physical or sexual abuse are all against the law. (Most people are not aware that assault is usually defined as a *perceived* threat of violence, not an actual violent act. If you or your child feel threatened, assault has occurred.) If you intend to press charges, police intervention is reasonable and necessary.

• **If the same behavior occurred between two adults, would it be a crime?** If you were locked in the bathroom for hours or stuffed into a dumpster at work, would you consider that assault and call the police? If so, the same standard holds for your child.

• **Is there a credible threat to your child's future safety?** Has the bully beaten or threatened to attack your child on his route to or from school or in some other public place? Has he been repeatedly threatened by a gang of older children or adolescents in your neighborhood? Are you aware of a "party house" in your area where unsupervised teenagers (including, perhaps, your child) may abuse alcohol or drugs and where violence frequently erupts? A crime does not have to have already occurred for you to call the police. In many cases policemen will be willing to talk with children or adolescents, warning them away from potentially criminal behavior, without making any arrests.

• **Is the harassment chronic? Have you tried other remedies without success?** If you have spoken with the bully, her parents and (if appropriate) her teacher and other school personnel, yet she continues to threaten, harass, attack or otherwise abuse your child, the police may be able to help you decide on an effective way to stop the behavior whether or not they contact the bully themselves.

When considering whether to contact the police on your child's behalf, keep in mind the police department's role as a community resource as well as enforcer of the law. Intervening in domestic disturbances, gang activity and other forms of interpersonal aggression among people who know each other has long been part of an officer's job description. Many have been specially trained in this type of service and can point you toward appropriate help even in cases when they cannot assist effectively themselves. Before you

call, however, be sure that you have gathered together as much information as possible to enable the police to help you: the names
and addresses of the bullies, exactly what happened, when and
where, a history of what you and your child have done so far to address the problems and the results, a list of any other agencies or
officials you have contacted about this issue and so on. Think ahead
of time about exactly what you want the police to do—talk to the
bully, contact her parents, mediate between the bully and your child
or arrest her.

It's also always best to discuss with your child your plans to contact the police. Many children are afraid of such contact and yours
may fear reprisal from the bully, embarrassment among his peers or
even negative attention from the police. Respect his concerns and
use this experience as an opportunity to demonstrate that the police
are here for our protection, not to "throw us in jail." It is highly instructive, in fact, for victimized children to see how quickly most
bullying stops once a uniformed policeman or other authority figure steps in. Such intervention may help demystify the legal process
for your child and encourage him to speak up and ask for help in the
future.

In most cases, police intervention serves as a one-time solution to
bullying—an emergency measure to solve a specific, serious problem. It does not generally address the underlying causes of your
child's victimization or the social patterns that have allowed the bullying to occur. While calling the police can make a life-or-death
difference for your child in some situations, it is important to consider long-term issues as well. Talking with the bully and his parents, seeking counseling for your child or accessing social services
or community support may all ensure your child's safety not only
today, but in the weeks, months and years to come.

"DOES MY CHILD
NEED LEGAL PROTECTION?"

Every child has the right to conduct her life without fear of being physically, emotionally or sexually abused. If you have tried to prevent your child's victimization by repeatedly contacting the bully's parents, school officials and the police, yet the harassment continues, you may have no choice but to take legal action against the bully and any institutions or adults who are responsible for your child's safety. If your child is being stalked or physically or sexually threatened, your first step can be to get a restraining order or an order of protection against the bully. A restraining order will make it illegal for the aggressor to come within a certain physical distance of your child and, if she does so, to risk arrest. Don't be afraid to contact your local police department, attorney or bar association for more information.

If the bully has already attacked your child, you may be in a position to file assault charges against him or to file a civil lawsuit. If the assault occurred at school after school officials had been made aware of the problem or if the bully had been disciplined previously, it may be possible to sue the school district or county as well, claiming that the school was negligent in its supervision and failed to protect one of its students. Holding the school system accountable in this way will not undo the harm that has already been done to your child, but it can provide her with the satisfaction of knowing that some form of justice has been done. It can also go a long way toward focusing more attention on the bullying problem at her and other schools. An increase in the number of such lawsuits has already led to the institution of schoolwide anti-bullying campaigns in a number of states. In the same way, civil lawsuits against the bullies themselves send an unambiguous message to their parents that imme-

diate action must be taken and alert others to the fact that adults
are responsible for all children's welfare. To locate an attorney in
your area who specializes in victim-abuse cases, call your local
bar association, or contact your nearest victims support group or
community action organization.

Indirect abuse—taunting, gossip-spreading and flaming on the
Internet—are more difficult to address through the legal system.
Most of these activities are protected by the First Amendment Free
Speech clause, though in some states charges of harassment may be
invoked against a bully who stalks or threatens another child by
telephone, mail or even the Internet. (A bully may also be subject to
arrest or prosecution if the speech involves a clear threat.) The use
of Internet message boards to spread cruel rumors or statements
about a child, painful as it can be, rarely leads to criminal prosecution. Such activity has been compared legally to a "slam book" or to
slurs scrawled on a bathroom wall—usually read by a limited group
of users and often accessible only by password, and so limited in the
damage it causes.

Victims of Internet flaming may consider filing a civil suit for
defamation of character or libel, since the legal definition of *libel*
applies to any published material that more than one person has
seen. Such suits are not always successful, however, since the defen-
dant may be able to prove that the use of a password strictly limited
access to the material, that the offensive statements were true (and
therefore not libelous) or that the writer was making use of his right
to free speech. To date, a more effective remedy has been disapproval from the bully's peers. As the effects of bullying become
better understood by students across the country, children and
teenagers will be more ready and eager to censure flaming they encounter on message boards and in chat rooms. Victims may also be
able to solicit information from these readers about who is doing
the flaming and how it might be stopped.

GOVERNMENT SANCTIONS, LAWS AND GUARANTEES

On November 2, 1998, a thirteen-year-old Georgia boy was fatally punched by his fifteen-year-old neighbor as the two got off the school bus near their homes. The killer had been suspended in the past for bullying and other infractions, yet no one had stopped the abuse. This terrible incident led to the 1999 signing of a statewide anti-bullying law by Georgia Governor Roy Barnes allowing schools to expel any student who has been disciplined at least three times for abusing others. Similar incidents, and the lawsuits that resulted, have inspired lawmakers in Texas, New York, Massachusetts and other states to support the creation of a wide range of anti-bullying legislation offering such remedies as early intervention and counseling as well as the automatic expulsion of offenders.

Such legislation works in much the same way that anti-bullying campaigns do in schools: it changes the social environment in ways that discourage violence and increases the chances that cruelty against others will be reported and stopped. Since a change in social climate has been shown to be one of the most effective remedies for bullying, it is certainly worth your while to support any such legislation and to encourage local lawmakers to pursue it. Contact your local anti-bullying activist group or community organization (see Resources, page 211) for more information on how you can help create laws to protect children everywhere from such violence.

COUNSELING, THERAPY AND OTHER PROFESSIONAL HELP

Whether your child has been victimized or is having trouble managing his aggressive impulses, counseling or therapy may lead to profound improvements in his behavior. Many children—particularly those who feel shame over their victimization or anger at being censured for aggression—resist talking to parents but are able to explore their situation with another, more objective adult. A trained counselor or therapist can help your victimized child work through his feelings of shame, confusion, depression or anger as well as work with him to curb any behaviors or attitudes that may lead bullies to single him out. She can also help an aggressive child explore the forces behind his anger and learn new, acceptable ways to channel it. Your school mental health professional can steer you toward reliable counselors or therapists in your area. Research has shown that the sooner bullies and victims are treated through reliable therapeutic techniques, the better the chances that they will learn to change their behavior and maintain their self-esteem. It may help to know that psychological treatment is often short-term. Though many families fear that treatment will last years, most cases can be addressed in a few sessions or a few months.

A number of therapeutic methods are commonly used to treat victims and perpetrators of childhood aggression. Your choice will depend on your child's needs, your family's approach to problem-solving and your therapist's recommendation. As you seek therapy for your child, you may be offered one or more of the following options:

Play Therapy. This technique, geared toward young children, employs a variety of play-related activities (puppets, painting pictures, etc.) to establish a relationship with the therapist in which problems can be addressed and resolved. Play therapy may help a child act out issues he feels uncomfortable speaking about, such as sexual abuse or physical bullying. It may also help a child see that domineering and controlling behavior may not get the best results when interacting with others.

Interpersonal Psychotherapy. The therapist and child engage in one-on-one conversation that focuses on the child's family relationships and current life. The goal is to use insights gained from these conversations to resolve problems and build on strengths. Interpersonal psychotherapy is especially helpful when a child doesn't understand why he's continually victimized, even when he tries to avoid bullies. The child may come to realize that he is sending subtle cues of which he was unaware.

Behavior Therapy. The focus of this approach is on changing specific unwanted behaviors through positive and negative reinforcements. Children also learn, through a process called desensitization, to decrease avoidance of situations that cause anxiety and discover how to manage them. This technique may enable a child to seek help from adults more easily or to stop exaggerating his degree of victimization.

Cognitive Therapy. This technique focuses on correcting distorted thinking patterns that lead to self-destructive or self-defeating behaviors. The aim is to replace negative thinking with more productive, positive messages. It is particularly effective with victimized children who become frightened before there is any reason to be, or aggressors who imagine a threat or insult when one wasn't intended.

Cognitive-Behavioral Therapy. This combination of cognitive and behavioral therapies helps children change negative thought patterns, behaviors and beliefs, thus relieving stress and leading more productive lives. A child may come to see that there are different ways of interpreting the same behavior and that a different interpretation may lead to a better result. He may also start to understand that it is possible to accomplish desired results (a stop to bullying, cessation of the other child's annoying behavior) in better ways.

Client-Centered Counseling. Based on the teachings of Carl Rogers, this approach begins with the assertion that the individual is the most knowledgeable about his own life. The therapist listens as the child sorts through his own ideas and choices, providing unconditional approval, empathy and attention. Client-centered counseling is especially useful for victimized children who are afraid to express their real fears, believing that doing so will make matters worse. The therapist provides support based on what the child really feels and helps him to generate his own solution.

Family Therapy. This technique focuses on the relationships and social dynamics within the family as the basis for examining and eventually changing individual behavior. Family therapy has been shown to have an especially positive effect in correcting aggressive behavior—not only in the bullying child but also in siblings who participate in therapy as well. It is most effective in addressing such family-related issues as sibling rivalry, parental stress, dominated siblings and similar situations. Families learn group strategies and focus on generating and maintaining more positive behaviors.

Group Therapy. The therapist meets with small groups of children or adolescents with similar problems, using the members' interactions to facilitate self-understanding and help them modify their behavior. Bullies and victims can begin to understand and change their behaviors by hearing firsthand about the behaviors of others and receiving honest feedback about their own words and actions. Group therapy also provides an opportunity to try out new ways of interacting and seeing the results.

Anger Management, Social Skills Training and Problem-Solving. These treatments, usually conducted in a group format, focus on techniques that children can use to manage their feelings, solve problems and interact constructively with their peers. Anger and frustration are frequently the cause of bullying. These treatments help reduce a child's level of anger and teach problem-solving skills, thus eliminating the need to bully or control another person. Group sessions may be held at school, in the community or through local mental health agencies.

Art Therapy. This focus on painting, drawing and other forms of art expression can be used to treat depression and trauma resulting from abuse. Art therapy provides a way for a relatively artistic child to communicate feelings of which he may not be consciously aware. Once the art has been produced, it provides an opportunity for expanded discussion. This technique is often used in conjunction with other therapies.

Dance/Movement Therapy. This technique focuses on integration of the "self" and achieving ease with one's own body. It can be especially effective with victims of physical, sexual or emotional abuse, since it fosters positive self-esteem.

Religious Counseling. You or your child may prefer to discuss his situation with a rabbi, priest or minister rather than a professional therapist. Such counselors are usually not trained to identify or treat mental health conditions such as depression or behavioral disorders, but they can help children work through problems with shame and anger, assure them that there is a higher power that supports them in doing the right thing, help bystanders deal with the moral issues involved in deciding whether or not to intervene, and refer families to appropriate social service agencies and professional services.

In some cases, a victim's or aggressor's experience with bullying stems in large part from a behavioral disorder such as ADHD (attention deficit/hyperactivity disorder), ODD (oppositional defiant disorder), and other developmental disorders or conditions such as depression or anxiety disorder. Children with ADHD frequently, through no fault of their own, provoke bullying responses by their difficulty controlling their behavior and style of social interaction. (They may pester the bully with questions, be physically intrusive or fail to respond to the aggressor's repeated attempts to get their attention.) Those with ODD can find it extremely difficult to compromise or to express themselves in nonaggressive ways, or they may have continuing problems with authority. Children who have been chronically bullied may exhibit symptoms of depression or anxiety that lead to more victimization or even suicidal thoughts.

If your child's teacher or guidance staff member spots any of the symptoms that may indicate these or other disorders, he may recommend that you have your child tested by a pediatrician or mental health professional. He may mention medication as a possible treatment to help your child moderate his behavior or emotions in ways that will lead to greater success and happiness at school.

Many parents find such a recommendation extremely distressing, since they feel it implies that there is "something wrong" with their child. In fact, these conditions occur quite frequently in the general population, and a child who has them *cannot help* behaving as he does. With properly prescribed medication and therapy, children with behavioral disorders and other conditions can improve their day-to-day lives in profound ways. If your child is referred for testing or diagnosis, try to keep an open mind as you search for the cause of his distress. Denying an existing problem only worsens the situation, while defining and accurately treating it can have the opposite effect.

Depression

Your child's teacher or school mental health professional may notice nothing unusual in your child's behavior, but you yourself may be wondering whether he needs professional help. Whether or not you are aware that your child has been the victim of chronic bullying, it is important to keep an eye out for signs of depression as he grows. (See the box on page 196 for a list of common symptoms.) Don't be afraid to ask him whether he is depressed or even whether he has been thinking about suicide. If his behavior indicates that this might be the case, your show of concern may be just the helping hand he's hoping for.

Whatever form of counseling or therapy you choose for your child, make a point of maintaining a positive attitude. You're taking positive steps to remedy his situation. There is nothing shameful or weak about seeking trained professionals to lead your child through an extremely difficult and complex aspect of his development. On the contrary, you can both be sure that he will emerge stronger and more competent thanks to their support. In the meantime, your efforts to find the best help for him will communicate your loving concern and your desire to help him lead a more positive, productive life.

WARNING SIGNS OF DEPRESSION

Chronic bullying is a major cause of depression in children and adolescents. When left untreated, depression can lead to extreme violence, suicide and other destructive actions. If you observe one or more of the following symptoms of depression, seek the help of a licensed psychologist or therapist:

- chronic sadness, tearfulness or crying
- hopelessness and pessimism
- violent behavior or destruction of property
- physical or sexual acting-out
- decreased interest in or inability to enjoy once-favorite activities
- low energy, persistent boredom
- social isolation, poor communication with family and friends
- low self-esteem and guilt
- extreme sensitivity to rejection or failure
- increased irritability, anger or hostility
- frequent complaints of physical illnesses, such as headaches and stomachaches, dizziness and nausea
- frequent absences from school or poor performance in school
- a major change in eating and/or sleeping patterns
- talk of or efforts to run away from home
- talk of suicide; self-mutilation or self-destructive behavior
- alcohol or drug abuse

FINDING SUPPORT IN YOUR COMMUNITY

Just as group and family therapy can be among the most effective ways for victims and aggressors to explore their bullying-related feelings and responses, so a community support group, youth group or even advocacy group can help both you and your child work through the complex reactions you have to your child's situation. Children and adolescents may experience a great deal of satisfaction participating in such groups as SAVE (Students Against Violence Everywhere). This grassroots organization consisting of more than 125 chapters nationwide offers anti-harassment and conflict-resolution programs to schools and promotes anti-bullying behavior in the community. Parents may become interested in joining an anti-bullying activist group such as Mothers Against Violence in America (MAVIA), an organization patterned after Mothers Against Drunk Driving. MAVIA, founded by the mother of a seventeen-year-old girl who was shot and killed by a nineteen-year-old, is dedicated to raising awareness of the effects of bullying and other violence in schools, in families, in society and in the media.

Parents of both victims and aggressors may start to wonder if the easy accessibility of firearms isn't one of the causes of extreme violence among today's children. Just as bleach, prescription medications and other potential poisons must be kept out of reach of young children in our homes, so guns and other weapons should be locked away from teenagers or even outlawed. The Violence Policy Center (VPC), a national organization working to reduce gun death and injury in America, seeks a ban on the most deadly category of firearms, the easily concealable handgun. A number of organizations are surfacing across the nation in support of similar aims.

If you are interested in becoming active in one of these or another support or activist organization, refer to Resources, page 211, for more information. Or consider starting your own group aimed at those issues you feel are most important. Your active community involvement can turn your distress over your child's bullying problems into productive action. What better behavior for your child to observe and imitate?

CHAPTER ELEVEN

DON'T WORRY: I TOOK CARE OF IT

"I KNOW HE DID. . . . He thinks he's so bad. . . . He called me a fag-got on the bus the other day. . . . He makes me wanna puke." When Diane heard her eleven-year-old son's half of this phone conversa-tion, it stopped her in her tracks. Bobby chattered on, unaware of his mother's presence behind him. "Yeah, right. Celia told me. He can say what he wants on his stupid Web site. Like I care."

Later that evening, after dinner, Diane knocked on Bobby's bed-room door. "Listen, I want to ask you something," she said tenta-tively after her son invited her in. "I happened to overhear you talking to Nat this afternoon. Are you have a problem with someone at school spreading rumors about you?"

As Diane had expected, Bobby looked surprised, then disapprov-ing of the idea that his mom had heard anything about his private life. But then he relaxed, and Diane was relieved to see that he didn't seem extremely upset. "No, Mom, it's okay," he said with a shrug. "There's this guy, Mick, who thinks he's a big deal at our school. He's trying to push me around. But I got my friends together and no one believes him. He's just making himself look bad."

"You're sure?" Diane asked. "Because, you know, that happened to me once when I was in junior high school. A girl in my class just got it into her head to spread all these rumors about me. It was the worst thing I ever went through in school."

"Nah, this isn't like that," Bobby reassured her. "I've got it under control, Mom. Don't worry."

Diane was indeed reassured, and pleased to see how confident her son appeared, even when his adolescent sexuality was brought into question. *I wish I'd been that sure of myself when I was his age*, she thought as she left her son's room. When Diane was young, she hadn't had anyone to talk to about problems with the other kids in school. It had never occurred to her parents to discuss how to handle other people's bullying or to stand up for herself. But Diane and Bobby had always talked about such things—discussing each other's feelings and points of view and evaluating the coping efforts they observed in television shows, in their own lives and in those of people they knew. Now, Diane could see, all those conversations were really paying off.

AIMING FOR SELF-SUFFICIENCY

One of the greatest pleasures of parenting is watching a child move from dependence toward full competency, a unique identity and self-realization. By guiding your child in appropriate ways at each stage of his development, you can help him learn to assert his rights and manage aggression successfully in himself and in others. Lessons and conversations introduced early in life can be adapted to other situations when he's older. By habitually naming and asking him to consider his own and others' emotions from early childhood on, you're equipping him with the skills to recognize and manage aggressive impulses later on. When you provide actual "scripts" with which to resolve conflict in kindergarten ("You can have it in just a minute, after I'm finished, okay?"), you powerfully demonstrate that there are ways to sidestep bullies even when there are no adults around. The same type of everyday guidance will also pave the way for satisfying adolescent conversations focusing not only on the fairness of relationships within your child's social group but the justice of political relationships in this country and around the world. Meanwhile, the habit of communicating with your child about such issues will help the two of you maintain a close relationship even through the stormy adolescent years.

You don't have to spend every minute of your time observing and commenting on your child's behavior to give him a solid education in emotional self-management and social skills. All that's needed is to make it a habit to think now and then about your child's social relationships and how he might improve them, and to incorporate ideas, suggestions and stories about relationships into his everyday life.

EXPANDING SELF-AWARENESS

Bullies are not the only people who feel angry. We all experience anger at times, but children who bully have not learned how to express their anger in nonaggressive ways. The first step for any parent trying to teach a child how to get along with others is to help her recognize and identify her own emotions, get to know what typically triggers them and encourage her to practice new ways of managing them.

An effective way to do this at any age, but especially when your child is very young, is to act as a mirror for your child, reflecting back to her the emotions you see. When you refuse to let her watch TV and she bursts into tears or tries to hit you, tell her how you think she feels ("I know you're angry") and identify the situation that has triggered this emotion ("It makes you mad when you want to do something and I say no, doesn't it?"). This expression of her emotion is deeply satisfying (and interesting) to your child, and she may stop crying or hitting in order to hear you talk about it. Now that you have her attention, you can help her find ways to manage her anger more successfully. ("But it doesn't help to cry or hit me. Hey—maybe we can make a compromise! Try asking me if you can watch one TV show after we've cleaned up your room.") As she grows familiar with this process, ask her to participate by suggesting a solution. ("You know that hitting people hurts them and gets you in trouble. And crying doesn't change anything. Can you think of a way to get what you want without hurting someone?")

Such remarks and observations are obvious to us as adults, but they are by no means obvious to our children. A child whose emotions are not verbally identified and explored in this way may never understand what is happening when a conflict sends her into a blinding rage. Again: such a child is not necessarily angrier than other children who do not slam locker doors on their "enemies' " hands or beat up smaller kids. She simply has not learned that what she is feeling is anger and that this is an emotion she can manage in less destructive ways. It should be clear, then, that identifying and talking about negative emotions is not just a nice thing for parents to do but a *necessary* first step in learning to live with others.

Identifying and exploring your child's emotions as they occur is only one way to help her understand her emotional experience. You can also remark on your own responses to certain situations, allowing her to examine the same emotions from a more objective point of view. ("When I haven't had enough sleep, I get cranky. I know it's going to be harder not to yell at people. Will you please remind me to count to ten?") Talk about others' emotional expressions and ask for your child's opinion on how well they managed the situation. ("Your brother was mad because he made a bad grade on his test. That made him feel bad about himself. But he shouldn't have yelled at you. What would you do if you were that mad?")

As your child moves through elementary school and junior high, encourage her to contribute more to these conversations. Whenever she describes her own or others' emotional reactions to events ("Miss Porper is so sarcastic to us. No one wants to speak up in class"), respond not only to the event (Miss Porper's sarcasm) but to the related emotional response (the kids' resistance). Discuss in an interested, involved but nonjudgmental way why the participants responded as they did ("Sarcasm makes you want to just curl up and protect yourself, doesn't it—and then you're not open to learning something new") and how the problem might be solved ("Maybe some of you could get together and write a letter to Miss Porper telling her how you feel").

Talk not only about ways to resolve conflicts but also how to channel aggressive emotions into acceptable forms. Encourage her to do something physical but nondestructive to work out her aggression (play a game of basketball, ride her bike, shut herself in her room with her CD player and dance). Help her get into the habit of expressing her feelings in creative ways (a journal, photography, painting, writing or performing in plays), and applaud the results no matter how "negative" they are. (Remind yourself that reading your daughter's play about a murderer is better than watching her act out her aggression in less creative ways!) Besides applauding, though, pay close attention to what your child is trying to say, and respond nonjudgmentally to that message, as you would if your child were a close friend. It is common for children who feel distressed to try to communicate their feelings creatively. A parent who hears what his child is saying can provide the support she may desperately need.

The older your child is, the more you can encourage her to do the analyzing as you discuss emotional situations and come up with solutions. Be sure to respond positively to her efforts, whatever they are, before you suggest improvements. By the time your child finishes high school, you may find that she's so familiar with this routine that she can resolve most such situations on her own, looking to you only occasionally for encouragement and advice. Her new independence indicates not an emotional separation from you but a new maturity—the welcome beginnings of adult self-sufficiency. Psychologists call this process a "scaffolding" approach, in which parents support their child just as scaffolding supports a building-in-progress—and then pull away the support bit by bit as the child becomes capable of supporting herself.

ENCOURAGING EMPATHY

Understanding others' emotions and their rights as individuals is not possible unless and until your child has learned to understand his own feelings. Yet self-understanding is not enough to ensure that your child will interact successfully with others. We all know people who are so wrapped up in their own emotional experience that they inadvertently "bully" others through neglect, selfishness or simple ignorance. You need to teach your child to look outward as well as inward, to consider and respect others' points of view and to respond appropriately to a wide variety of emotional expressions.

The way to do this, again, is to put the emotions into words. At around age three or four, children begin to realize that others have feelings, too, and that these emotions or viewpoints are not necessarily in line with their own. This is a fascinating discovery for young children, and you can enhance your child's understanding by identifying and discussing the emotions the two of you observe in others. ("Look how that little boy is frowning. He must be sad. I guess he didn't like it when his mom made him give that girl her truck back. What should he do now—go make a sand castle with that other boy?") It helps to relate others' feelings to your child's ("It's hard to give a toy back when you want to play with it, isn't it? Did you ever feel that way?") and to let him know that you have felt that way yourself. ("I have a hard time giving Dad back the remote control for the TV. Did you see how he had to ask me twice for it yesterday? But then, after he changed the channels, I decided to play a board game with you and we had a great time.")

Books, movies, TV shows and real-life accounts offer other ways to talk about others' feelings from early childhood through late adolescence and into adulthood. You might start out simply identifying emotions ("Look, the girl on that page is smiling. Do you think she's happy?"), then compare your child's feelings and those of the story characters ("Who do you think is most like you in this story?"), and experiment with conflict resolution and other social problem-solving skills. ("How do you think Leah felt when Renata called her stupid? What could Leah have done?") As your child grows older, encourage him to tell you about relationships among his peers and how conflicts are resolved. (Preteens and adolescents are fully focused on this issue and will eagerly talk about it if you refrain from criticizing and simply listen.) As you talk about these situations, ask your child how he thinks each party felt, whether he has ever been in a similar position or felt the same way, and how he thinks the problem could have best been solved. Be sure to match his confidences with some of your own. Stories you tell him about your own encounters with frustration or bullying convey the powerful message that everyone encounters such situations and must resolve them as best they can.

Empathy can also be taught by example, and it is important to consider the impact that your own attitudes have on your child's ability to consider and cope with others' feelings. Your child will observe and imitate your responses to his own behavior, treating others with respect if that's the way you treat him. The same goes for your attitude toward those outside the family. Your child will note your efforts to help your neighbors, give to those less fortunate and sympathize with others' distress. He will also notice and imitate your willingness to do so. Many parents wish their teenaged children would rechannel some of their restless energy into doing good deeds for the less fortunate people in the world. If you feel this way about your adolescent, consider volunteering yourself, and afterward describe some of your experiences. When an opportunity arises for your child to participate, mention it to him. Teenagers' natural idealism can prompt even the toughest kids to "mentor" younger children or help the elderly, and such experiences can vastly expand their ability to understand and tolerate others.

COMMUNICATION AND SHARING

Much of this book has emphasized the importance of keeping the lines of communication open to help your child learn to cope with challenging social situations. Most parents understand that maintaining communication requires listening to their child in an empathetic, nonjudgmental, accepting way. It is equally important, however, for parents to talk to their children—to share their own experiences just as they expect their children to share theirs. By asking a child of any age "What would you do if you were me?" or "That makes me so mad. Do you ever feel that way?" you invite your child into your world and demonstrate your respect for her opinion. As with our adult friends, this type of two-way relationship leads to much richer, fuller communication than concentrating on only one person's concerns.

During the early years, the focus will necessarily remain much more on your child's experiences than on your own. You and your child will spend a great deal of time identifying her emotions and discussing the behaviors that result. Still, young children are thrilled to be asked for an opinion. Your occasional questions ("Daddy wants half of my apple, but I'm so hungry I don't want to share. What should I do?") are a powerful way to get her thinking about how people cope with conflict. During middle childhood, when your child is likely to become quite interested in what you were like at her age, your descriptions of your past and current experiences can help her understand that she is not the only person on earth to feel scared, frustrated or intimidated by others. They can also help instill a level of trust that will carry the two of you through the adolescent years.

Adolescents, self-involved by nature, may be somewhat less interested in hearing about your feelings. Still, a history of mutual sharing will help her understand your point of view as you monitor her activities and otherwise meet your responsibilities as a parent. She may also trust you more to help her manage any bullying situations that occur or even to step in. Meanwhile, it is a good idea to increase the number of times you ask your teenager for advice. Such reality-check questions ("You think I handled that okay?") keep your relationship alive at a time when children are especially sensitive to one-sided interrogations and other parental demands.

Humor is another technique that parents may forget to use when maintaining relationships with their children. Using a joke to resolve a conflict or frustration between your child and yourself can ease a potentially negative experience and demonstrates a new way she can manage conflict herself. If you find yourself yelling at your child the minute he walks into the house ("Barry, I want to know why you came home so late last night!"), temper your reaction with a humorous acknowledgment. ("Uh-oh, I just remembered, my dad used to ask me that all the time. I thought he was such a stupid idiot. I don't really want to be an idiot. I'm just worried about you.") Laughing at yourself and then explaining how you feel goes a long way toward enabling your child to trust and confide in you.

All of these techniques for improving communication—listening nonjudgmentally, contributing your own stories and observations and using humor to ease conflict and encourage confidence—are aimed at making it easier for your child to come to you when bullying occurs. A child who has grown up observing her parents listen carefully, respect others' viewpoints and manage conflict gracefully is also better prepared to deal with bullying on her own.

PROVIDING LIMITS AND SUPPORT

As we have seen throughout this book, children need to know that their feelings and desires are accepted by others, but they also need to know that there are clear limits to the ways in which they may express those emotions. Stating clearly what those limits are, and consistently providing logical consequences when they are transgressed, is one of the best ways for you to teach your child to interact with others successfully. Your child needs to know that hurting others is not acceptable—whether he or another child is doing the hurting—and that reporting these behaviors to adults will bring an end to them.

Your first step in providing this type of support is to divide up your young child's world into what is "his" and what is "yours"—what he is allowed and not allowed to do, what he may control and what you must have power over. Where you place your limits is, to a large degree, up to you. More important is that you enforce limits consistently by imposing reasonable consequences. You may explain to your preschooler, for example, that it's okay to hug another child, but he must stop if the child says no. If he doesn't stop, he will not be allowed to play with that child for a while. This rule must then be enforced each time your child transgresses, no matter what the reason. You can set a good example of managing emotions by enforcing the rule without getting angry or upset and by calmly putting the consequence into effect. ("Okay, Trevor, Lindy said no and you kept hugging her, so you have to stop playing with her now. Let's go look at these blocks.") As your child enters kindergarten and elementary school, invite him to suggest rules, along with the consequences for breaking them. (You may have to tone down his ideas to some degree. Given the chance, most children are stricter than their parents.) Not only does this get your child thinking about why we need such rules, but he is likely to resist the rules less if he helped create them. He may also respond well to conversations about alternative behaviors that can help him stay within his limits more successfully, such as spending time alone in his room rather than yelling when he feels grumpy, or going to an adult when he's threatened instead of punching another child.

If you consistently enforce limits, your child will probably respect them most—though certainly not all—of the time. Such self-monitoring is clearly necessary in learning to manage his own aggression (he must learn that he can't hit people when he's angry), but it is also vital for learning how to respond to others' aggressive behavior. A child who "knows the rules"—who has tested your limits and experienced roughly the same results every time—understands that he need not be victimized by anyone. When threatened, he will be much more likely to turn to you or another adult to enforce logical consequences, and he will have a clearer idea of which types of behavior are unacceptable. He will even make a more effective "bystander" as he acts on his knowledge that, for example, no one's personal space should be violated and no one should be called names.

SPENDING TIME TOGETHER

Perhaps the most powerful method for increasing your child's self-confidence and self-awareness is to simply spend as much time with him as possible. We all know that the world these days is a very busy place and parents have lots of important things to do—yet spending more time together is the number one solution to helping families under stress. It is not necessary to jam-pack your time together with

activities or intense conversations. From infancy through adulthood, just hanging out, watching TV together, or having dinner
still lets your child know that you care enough to want to spend time
with him. During your child's early years, this casual contact is the
best way to learn about his life when he's away from you, since it is
difficult for him to consciously recall and frame such information
when asked directly. As he approaches adolescence, he urgently requires the benefit of your example, empathy and support—even if
he acts as if he doesn't want to be with you. No matter what you are
doing with your child, he will observe your ways of interacting with
others and use your example to help him through his own everyday
encounters. Be aware that he is watching and remembering what
you do and say, and provide him with good ideas for coping with his
own and others' aggression.

STAYING FLEXIBLE

The idea of implementing all of these concepts throughout childhood may seem overwhelming at first. But instilling a feeling of
confidence and security in your child, and educating her in how to
manage aggression in herself and others, does not have to be a full-
time job. At its best, social education is more a matter of attitude
than constant, conscious vigilance—an attitude that surfaces in a variety of ways in your everyday interactions.

   In my talks at schools and in the media, and in my conversations
with clients, I encourage parents to consider the fact that learning
to deal with bullies is as easy as learning your vowels. Each vowel
represents an idea that can help you in designing your basic parenting approach:

   A = maintaining **awareness** that bullying takes place all the
        time
   E = periodically **evaluating** the progress your child has made in
        stopping bullying

I = **intervening** in ways that empower your child and teach her how to manage future conflicts on her own

O = **observing** on a daily basis how your child feels and how well she is managing her life

U = **understanding** your child by communicating freely with her as an individual who deserves your respect and confidence

And sometimes Y = remembering that **young** people sometimes think and behave differently from adults and need to be approached in ways that are appropriate to their level of development. Young people have a right to safety and protection, just as adults do. Remember, if it's a crime when an adult does it, it's a crime when a child does it even though he may not be legally responsible.

By keeping in mind these general concepts, rather than a list of hard-and-fast rules, you can remain open to your child's particular circumstances, personality and needs at any stage in her development. More than anything, teaching your child to manage bullying is a way of helping her to better understand herself and others. Remaining flexible—observing your child for who she is, considering the probable consequences of her actions and steering her toward more positive behaviors in any way that works—is the best approach for any parent who dreams of helping his child lead a happy, bully-free life. The more you *enjoy* your child, responding fully to each new pleasure and challenge as it occurs, the more secure she will feel and the better able she'll be to treat others with kindness and respect.

RESOURCES

BOOKS FOR PARENTS

Faber, Adele, and Elaine Mazlish, *Siblings Without Rivalry: How to Help Your Children Live Together So You Can Live Too* (expanded edition). New York: Avon Books, 1998.

Faber, Adele and Elaine Mazlish, *How to Talk So Kids Will Listen & Listen So Kids Will Talk* (20th anniversary edition). New York: Avon Books, 1999.

Hoover, John H., and Ronald Oliver, *The Bullying Prevention Handbook: A Guide for Principals, Teachers, and Counselors*. Bloomington, Ind.: National Educational Service, 1996. Contact: National Educational Service, 1252 Loesch Rd., Bloomington, IN 47402; (812) 336-7700 or (800) 733-6786.

Olweus, Dan, *Bullying at School: What We Know and What We Can Do*. Oxford, England: Blackwell Publishers, 1993. Contact: Blackwell Publishers, P.O. Box 20, Williston, VT 05495; (800) 216-2522.

Ross, Dorothea M., *Childhood Bullying and Teasing: What School Personnel, Other Professionals, and Parents Can Do*. Alexandria, VA: American Counseling Association, 1996.

Zimbardo, Philip G., *Shyness: What It Is, What to Do About It*. New York: Addison-Wesley, 1990.

BOOKS FOR CHILDREN

Berenstain, Stan, and Jan Berenstain, *The Berenstain Bears and the Bully*. New York: Random House, 1993.

Brown, Marc, *Arthur's April Fool*. Boston: Little, Brown & Company, 1983.

Golding, William, *Lord of the Flies*. New York: Prentice Hall, 1959.
Excellent reading for adolescents, this classic novel explores the natural tendency toward aggression that all humans experience. This book can spark fascinating discussions with your teenager about the nature of violence and how children and teenagers can and must be taught different ways to interact.

Shriver, Maria, *What's Wrong with Timmy?* New York: Warner Books, 2001.
Helps children understand peers who are different and have special needs. An excellent tool for teaching lessons about acceptance.

Walker, Alice, *Finding the Green Stone*. San Diego: Harcourt Brace Jovanovich, 1991.

Webster-Doyle, Terrence, *Why Is Everybody Always Picking on Me? A Guide to Understanding Bullies for Young People*. Middlebury, Vt.: Atrium Society Publications, 1991.

ON-LINE SUPPORT

www.bbc.co.uk/education/archive/bully/

Web site for the report *Bullying: A Survival Guide*, from Britain's BBC Education.

www.bullybeware.com

Bully B'ware: Take Action Against Bullying. An excellent meeting place for parents, children and educators concerned about bullying and its effects. Provides current research on bullying, information on school programs and other resources and opportunities for victims and bullies to discuss their own experience with peer violence.

www.bullying.org

A clearinghouse of information on bullying and services for victims and aggressors.

www.ed.gov

Information on stopping bullying at school. Offers the government publication "Creating Safe and Drug-Free Schools: An Action Guide."

www.familyfun.com

Helpful information on all aspects of parenting, including managing aggression in children.

www.GLSEN.org

GLSEN is the leading national organization fighting to end anti-gay bias in K-12 schools.

www.healthyplace.com

The nation's largest mental health Web site. Comprehensive information on mental health services and therapeutic approaches to violence and victimization in children and adolescents.

www.home-school.com

A source of information on homeschooling programs and curricula, along with support and information for parents considering or continuing with homeschooling their children.

www.kidshelp.org

Provides referrals to anti-bullying groups and resources in your area. Includes a monitored kids' chat room as well as an on-line counselor.

www.pesten.net/index_English.html

An on-line source of support for victims of aggression.

www.surgeongeneral.gov/library/youthviolence/youvioreport.htm

Web site for the report *Youth Violence: A Report of the Surgeon General.* Created in response to the shooting at Colorado's Columbine High School, this comprehensive report on the state of bullying in America today includes evaluations of current anti-bullying programs, therapeutic approaches for violent and victimized youths, and many other resources for parents and children interested in learning more about bullying in the United States.

www.teasingvictims.com

A supportive and informative Web site for young victims of bullying.

http://youthviolence.edschool.virginia.edu

Research and support for professionals and parents regarding youth violence.

www.vpc.org

The Violence Police Center is a national organization working to reduce gun death and injury in the U.S.

SUPPORT ORGANIZATIONS AND HOTLINES

American Foundation for Suicide Prevention (888) 333-2377
Covenant House Youth Crisis Hotline (800) 999-9999
Focus Adolescent Services (877) FOCUS-AS (362-8727)
National Domestic Violence Hotline (800) 799-7233; for the hearing impaired: (800) 787-3224
National Mental Health Association (800) 969-6642
National Referral Network for Kids in Crisis (800) KID-SAVE (543-7283)
National Runaway Switchboard (800) 621-4000
Trevor Helpline for Gay, Lesbian and Bisexual Youth (800) 850-8078

INDEX

helping the victim, 109, 115–28,
190–94
identifying problem, 142–44
media and, 111–12
by parents, 95–97, 125–26, 127,
139–81
peer pressure in, 110–13
recognizing bullying, 7–8, 10,
56–57, 100–103, 107–8
rehearsal of response, 118,
122–23, 135, 199–200
safety of, 105–7, 148–49
at school. *See* school-based
intervention
self-sufficiency as goal of,
199–200, 203
support of other adults in, 64, 93,
106, 108–9, 120, 124, 136,
143–44, 177
talking with bully, 91–94, 109–10,
128–38, 143, 144–48, 190–94
talking with parents of bully,
140–42, 145, 148–55
talking with victim and parents of
victim, 63–72, 143–44, 156–58
by witnesses, 95–97, 103–7
intimidation, 47
isolation, of victims, 13, 32, 60–61,
74–75, 101, 109

jealousy, 129
jokes, practical, 32, 36, 43
jostling, social, 6–7, 12–13
judgments, avoiding, 151–52, 159

Kidscape, 59
kindergarten bullying, 6
forms of, 100
physical abuse, 38
recognizing, 100, 107
social abuse, 43–44
verbal abuse, 40

labeling, 6, 47, 71–72, 100, 179
legal protection, 26, 187–89
legislation, anti-bullying, 3, 189
libel, 188

limits, providing, 207–8
listening
basic skills in, 134
to bullies, 91–94, 157–58
to others' comments about your
child, 65, 81–84, 156–58
to victims of bullying, 10, 13,
66–72, 143–44, 156–58
See also information-gathering
stage; talking
locker room bullying, 54, 169
lunchroom bullying, 169, 174

makeovers, 127
mass shootings, 2, 22
master-apprentice approach,
144–46, 150
MAVIA (Mothers Against Violence
in America), 196–97
mediation, 174
medication, 194
meetings, 148–56
failure of, 159–60
following up on, 155
making contact, 149–50
with parents of bully, 148–55
with parents of victim, 156–58
positive conclusion to, 152–54
simplicity of, 151–52
with teachers and school officials,
176–77
See also talking
middle school bullying
forms of, 102
impact of, 21–23
physical abuse, 38
questions to uncover, 69
recognizing, 102–3, 108
school-based intervention and,
166
sexual abuse, 46–47
status of bullies in, 74, 76
verbal abuse, 40–41
molestation, 19
Mothers Against Violence in
America (MAVIA), 196–97
motivation, of bully, 116

ABOUT THE AUTHOR

PETER L. SHERAS, PH.D., is a clinical psychologist and professor of education in the Curry Programs in Clinical and School Psychology at the University of Virginia in Charlottesville, Virginia. He is associate director of the Virginia Youth Violence Project and co-coordinator of the local school crisis network. He specializes in understanding school violence and its prevention and works extensively with school-age children and their families in treatment. He is coauthor of the *Stress Index for Parents of Adolescents*.

Dr. Sheras holds a diplomate in clinical psychology from the American Board of Professional Psychology and is a past president of the Virginia Psychological Association. He is married to clinical psychologist Phyllis Koch-Sheras, with whom he coauthored *The Dream Sharing Sourcebook*, a book about creating positive relationships. He has two children, Daniel and Sarah, both now young adults.